To my wife, Kristie

You are my anchor and my wings, my steady river and my open sky. Through every season, you have shown me the power of grace, the beauty of resilience, and the joy of walking hand in hand. You remind me every day that love is not just a feeling— it's a choice, a commitment, and a legacy. This book is for you From this day forward.

PREFACE

Now, let's imagine James and Maria as the perfect union of two vastly different creatures, a bird and a hippopotamus. Why these two? Because their dynamic is a picture of how God uses differences to bring balance, depth, and beauty to marriage.

The bird is light, agile, and full of dreams. It can soar to great heights, see the bigger picture, and fly from one idea to the next with energy and excitement. In marriage, the bird represents creativity, spontaneity, and optimism. This is the partner who says, Let's take a leap of faith! and who reminds the hippo to look up from the ground once in a while and see the sky. But sometimes, the bird's lofty flights can feel aimless. Without direction, it risks losing its way, or its purpose.

The hippo is solid, grounded, and steady. It's slow to move but immensely powerful when it does. In marriage, the hippo represents strength, stability, and practicality. This is the partner who says, Let's think this through first, and who provides a firm foundation when life gets unpredictable. But sometimes, the hippo's grounded nature can make it resistant to change, overly cautious, or stuck in routines.

FOREWARD

I make the choice to love you everyday.
The same choice I made in the beginning.
Your love smoothed the jagged edges of my soul
And repaired the cracks in my heart that needed mending.

If it's truly darkest before the dawn...
Then on the stormiest nights,
I'll always stay.
God gave you to me.
Your father gave me a gift
that I could never turn away.

For Richer or Poorer
Through Sickness or health
I die to my pride.
I die to myself.
I can't promise forever.
I promise you now.
I'll walk through the fire.
Never throw in the towel
I'll cover you!!!
Even if my arms can't carry the weight.
I'll do all I can
No matter what it takes.

This I will do
As we sail through this life
Troubling times we may shoulder.
I can only go one way with you....

Forward...From this day....Forward.

FOREWARD

TABLE OF CONTENTS

FOREWARD — 4

PREFACE — 8

Chapter 1 It's Not Good for Man to Be Alone... And Don't We Know It! — 11

Chapter 2 Marriage Is Like a Lifetime Warranty... but Better — 21

Chapter 3 Who's the King, Who's the Queen, and Who Keeps Eating the Royal Ice Cream? — 33

Chapter 4 Two Are Better Than One, Unless You're Sharing a Blanket — 53

Chapter 5 Praying for Your Spouse, Even When You Want to Pray About Them Instead — 61

Chapter 6 It's Not Your Money or My Money, It's God's Money. — 83

Chapter 7 Can You Hear Me Now? — 97

Chapter 8 No Respect, No Rhythm — 108

Chapter 9 Building a Life Without Losing Yourself — 122

Chapter 10 Your Love Is the Sermon Everyone's Watching — 132

Chapter 11 Because the World Needs More Leaders (and Fewer Juice Boxes) — 144

Chapter 12 The Theater vs. The Director's Cut — 159

Chapter 13 Why Your Love Language Lied to

You (and Why That's a Good Thing)	168
Chapter 14 From This Day Forward	180
Conclusion	187
About The Author	189

PREFACE

Marriage: a word brimming with promise, hope, and sometimes, a little trepidation. It's the intertwining of two lives, two hearts, and often, two very different approaches to life. For centuries, couples have walked down the aisle, full of love and expectation, only to discover that building a thriving marriage is less like a fairy tale and more like an adventure—one that requires grit, grace, and a good sense of humor.

This book is not about finding the perfect marriage; it's about forging a meaningful one. It's for the couple standing at the altar, ready to say "I do," and for those who've been in the trenches of matrimony for years, wondering if they can make it work. It's for the spouse who feels unseen, the partner who feels unappreciated, and the pair who are struggling to remember why they started this journey together in the first place. Most of all, it's for anyone who believes that love—real, resilient, and sometimes messy—can triumph with the right tools and a willing heart.

Through the lens of the hippo and the bird, two unlikely partners who learn to navigate life's rivers together, this book offers practical insights, spiritual wisdom, and honest reflections on the realities of marriage. The hippo represents strength, stability, and practicality. The bird embodies vision, spontaneity, and optimism. Together, they are a reminder that marriage thrives not in sameness but in the harmony of differences.

From understanding how to celebrate each other's unique gifts to navigating the inevitable conflicts with grace, this book dives into what it takes to create a partnership that lasts. It's about learning to dance together—sometimes with rhythm, sometimes with a few missteps, but always with purpose. As you turn these pages, you'll find stories that resonate, lessons that inspire, and challenges that encourage growth. But most importantly, you'll find hope.

Hope that no matter where you are in your marital journey, there's always room for deeper connection, greater understanding, and the kind of love that reflects God's design. Marriage isn't about avoiding the hard times; it's about facing them together. It's about holding hands through the storms, building bridges across the rivers, and finding joy in the journey. My prayer is that this book becomes a guide, a comfort, and an inspiration as you work to make your marriage not just good, but great. Let's embark on this journey together—from this day forward.

TIMOTHY HUNTER

CHAPTER 1

It's Not Good for Man to Be Alone...
And Don't We Know It!

Imagine Adam, the very first man, standing in the middle of Eden. He's surrounded by every living creature God could dream up. He's got lions, lambs, and maybe even a dodo bird strolling by. But despite being in a literal paradise, Adam scratches his head and thinks, "Is this it? I'm supposed to spend eternity hanging out with a giraffe?" Cue God looking down and saying the most relatable line in human history, "It's not good for man to be alone." (Genesis 2:18)

And thus, the prototype for humanity's favorite dynamic duo, husband and wife, was born. But let's be real, marriage doesn't always feel like paradise. Sometimes, it feels like a crash course in communication with subtitles that don't quite match the dialogue.

The Popasal That Almost Wasn't

Meet James and Maria. James, a numbers guy with spreadsheets for everything, had planned their proposal down to the millisecond. Maria, a free spirit who thought schedules were optional, loved James for his predictability until it started to drive her nuts. On the night James planned to propose, Maria, as usual, was running late.

"Babe," James said, pacing the living room, ring box burning a hole in his pocket, " we're going to miss the reservation."

Maria rolled her eyes. "It's just dinner, not the Second Coming."

James muttered under his breath, "You'll be saying that until the breadsticks run out."

By the time Maria was ready, James was sweating like he'd just run a marathon. They got to the restaurant, and everything was perfect, candlelight, soft music, appitizers, the works! But when James got down on one knee and started his heartfelt speech, Maria burst out laughing.

"Oh my gosh, you're so nervous! You're like a squirrel in traffic!" she giggled, not realizing he was trying to propose.

James froze, stunned into silence ad confusion. This was not how it looked in his spreadsheet. But as he fumbled for words, Maria caught on and gasped.

"Oh! Are you... Wait, yes! YES! YES, I DO!" she yelled, loud enough to make the entire restaurant clap.

One day, the bird was fluttering about, dreaming of flying across the river to explore the lush fields on the other side. "Let's go!" the bird chirped enthusiastically. "There's so much to see over there!" The hippo, munching intensely on grass, looked up and said, "We can't just leave. What if the river's too deep? What if the grass isn't greener over there? We should stay here, where it's safe."

At first, the bird thought, "Why is the hippo so boring?" and the hippo thought, "Why is the bird so reckless?" But after some discussion, they came up with a plan: the bird would scout the area from above, and the hippo would use its strength to help them cross safely. Together, they reached the other side, exploring new opportunities while staying grounded in wisdom.

The bird and the hippo teach us that marriage isn't about finding someone exactly like you—it's about finding someone who complements you. One partner's strength can balance the other's weakness, and their differences can create a partnership greater than the sum of its parts. Ecclesiastes 4:9-12 puts it perfectly:

Two are better than one because they have a good return for their labor. If either of them falls down, one can help the other up.

The bird needs the hippo's stability, and the hippo needs the bird's vision. Together, they embody God's design for companionship, a union that thrives on collaboration, mutual respect, and shared goals.

James's spreadsheets needed Maria's spontaneity, and Maria's carefree spirit needed James's structure. Together, they balanced each other, just like Adam needed Eve to balance his life in the garden. God knew from the start that human beings aren't wired to do life alone. We need someone who sees our blind spots and loves us anyway.

Dating Was the Test Run

Before James and Maria tied the knot, they went through the great trial known as premarital road trips. If you've ever been in a car with someone for more than three hours, you know it's a crash course in patience, conflict resolution, and snack compatibility. James once pulled over to consult Google Maps for a better route, and Maria joked, "You're taking directions from an algorithm, and I'm the one with no sense of direction?"

"Maria," he replied, gripping the steering wheel like it owed him some money, "you literally just said, 'Turn left where the cows are smiling.'"

Somehow, they made it to their destination without needing a marriage counselor. But that road trip taught them more about each other than any date night ever could. It revealed James's need for control and Maria's need for spontaneity, and how they'd need to work together to make it all work.

When God created Eve, He didn't just whip her up as an afterthought. The Bible says God made Eve from Adam's rib, not from his head to rule over him, or from his feet to be beneath him, but from his side, equal, close to his heart. That's not just poetic; it's a blueprint. A marriage where both partners work together as equals reflects God's design.

James and Maria didn't get everything right, no one ever does, but they started to see how their differences could become their strengths. Where James saw risk, Maria saw opportunity. Where Maria saw chaos, James saw a plan.
Together, they were better than they ever could have been alone.

God's design for your story

Let's circle back to Adam. He didn't know what he was

missing until God presented him with Eve. And when he saw her, he didn't say, "Oh cool, another human." He said, "This is now bone of my bones and flesh of my flesh" (Genesis 2:23). In other words, "Finally, someone who gets me!"

Marriage isn't about finding someone who's perfect. It's about finding someone who helps you grow, challenges you, and loves you through the messy, unscripted moments of life. Whether you're single, dating, or married, remember: God's design for companionship isn't just about solving loneliness, it's about building something beautiful together.

Even if James and Maria's road trip tested their patience, it was just the beginning of their adventure. Marriage, like life, is less about the destination and more about who's in the passenger seat with you.

Chapter 1 Reflection Questions

How has God used relationships (romantic or otherwise) to teach you about yourself?

If you're single, what traits are you asking God for in a partner? How might they complement your own strengths and weaknesses?

If you're married, how can you celebrate the ways your differences make your partnership stronger?

CHAPTER 2

Marriage Is Like a Lifetime
Warranty... but Better

It's a bright, sunny Saturday, and Kyle and Jasmine are standing at the altar. Jasmine is glowing, Kyle's palms are sweating, and the pastor is halfway through for better or for worse when Kyle sneaks a glance at Jasmine and whispers, "We've got this, right?" Jasmine smirks and whispers back, "I'm not saying I signed up for worse, but... I'm ready."

The audience chuckles softly, but little do Kyle and Jasmine know that in about two years, "for worse," it will look like Kyle setting the kitchen on fire, attempting to cook a romantic dinner. Jasmine will yell, "You can't sauté water!" and Kyle will reply, "Why didn't anyone warn me that marriage doesn't come with smoke detectors?"

Not just a Pretty Contract

A lot of people treat marriage like a contract, I'll do my part as long as you do yours. But the Bible says marriage is a covenant, not a contract. What's the difference? A contract is based on mutual convenience; a covenant is built on mutual sacrifice.

Here's the thing about covenants: they're meant to hold up even when the other person doesn't. That's why they're sacred. God didn't make His covenant with humanity contingent on us keeping all our promises. He made it because He loves us enough to stick with us even when we don't deserve it.

Let me illustrate this with Kyle and Jasmine again. One day, Kyle accidentally breaks Jasmine's favorite coffee mug, the one with #1 Wife, written on it in gold letters. Jasmine, who cherishes that mug, stares at the shattered pieces on the floor and takes a deep breath.

Kyle panics. "I'll buy you a new one!" he blurts out.

But Jasmine shakes her head. "Kyle, it's not about the mug. It's about what the mug meant. It's my favorite because you gave it to me."

Kyle, seeing the disappointment in her eyes, realizes it's not about replacing the mug, it's about restoring trust. So, instead of rushing to Amazon, he grabs the broken pieces and painstakingly glues them back together. It's not perfect, but Jasmine smiles when she sees his effort. The mug is a little cracked, but it's whole, and so is their bond.

Marriage is like that coffee mug. It's not about keeping it pristine and perfect, it's about being willing to pick up the broken pieces and work to put them back together. A contract would say, "Let's just replace it." A covenant says, "Let's fix it, no matter what it takes."

In every marriage, there are moments when something cherished gets broken, not always physically, but emotionally or relationally. The coffee mug is a simple yet profound reminder that what matters most in these moments isn't perfection or quick fixes, but intentionality and care.

Recongizing The Break

When Kyle broke Jasmine's favorite coffee mug, it wasn't

just about the object itself. For Jasmine, that mug represented more than a vessel for her morning coffee, it carried sentimental value. It was a symbol of Kyle's love, thoughtfulness, and their shared bond.

In every marriage, there are things we hold dear, shared traditions, trust, or little tokens of love. When those things are shattered, whether through a mistake, a misunderstanding, or even neglect, it can feel deeply personal. The pain isn't always about the object or the action, it's about what it represents.

Kyle's first instinct was to offer a replacement. "I'll buy you a new one!" he exclaimed, thinking a fresh, unbroken mug would solve the problem. But here's the lesson: in relationships, quick fixes don't heal.

Jasmine's response "It's not about the mug; it's about what the mug meant", reveals a deeper truth. What we often crave in moments of hurt isn't substitution but restoration. It's not about finding a perfect replacement; it's about honoring the value of what was broken and showing that it still matters.

Glueing the Pieces Together

Instead of defaulting to convenience, Kyle took the harder route. He gathered the broken pieces and carefully glued them back together. It was tedious, imperfect work. The cracks were visible, but so was the effort, and it spoke volumes.

The repair wasn't about fixing a mug, it was about restoring something more significant: trust and connection. Jasmine didn't smile because the mug looked flawless; she smiled because Kyle showed her that she and what mattered to her was worth his time, effort, and care.

This is the essence of marital restoration. When trust, intimacy, or a shared value is broken, it's not about pretending it never happened or replacing it with something new. It's about putting in the effort to acknowledge the damage, take responsibility, and work together to make it whole again.

The Beauty of the Cracks

The repaired mug, with its visible cracks, became a new kind of symbol for Kyle and Jasmine. It wasn't perfect, but it was whole. In many ways, it was even more valuable than before because it told a story, not just of love, but of redemption.

In marriage, those cracks are inevitable. Mistakes will happen, misunderstandings will arise, and things will occasionally fall apart. But when we choose to repair instead of replace, those cracks become part of the story, reminding us of the strength and resilience that love brings.

There's even a parallel here with the Japanese art of Kintsugi, where broken pottery is repaired with gold, making the cracks a feature, not a flaw. The philosophy behind Kintsugi teaches that brokenness doesn't reduce an object's value, it enhances it. Similarly, in marriage, the process of repairing and restoring can deepen love and connection, making the relationship even more meaningful.

God's Covenant vs. Human Promises

God's covenant with us is the ultimate example of this. Look at Abraham in Genesis 15. When God made a covenant with Abraham, He told him to prepare an offering, then caused Abraham to fall into a deep sleep. While Abraham was sleeping, God alone passed through the offering, symbolizing that He would uphold the covenant, even if Abraham didn't.

In the same way, marriage calls us to a higher standard.

When we say I do, we're not just making a promise to our spouse; we're making a promise to God. And God doesn't take promises lightly (Ecclesiastes 5:4-5).

The coffee mug challenges us to think about how we respond when something precious in our marriage gets broken. Do we rush to find a quick fix, hoping to gloss over the issue? Or do we take the time to acknowledge the hurt, understand its meaning, and work together to repair what was lost?

Kyle's decision to glue the pieces back together is a reminder that the effort we put into restoring what's broken, whether it's trust, respect, or love, carries far more weight than a flawless replacement ever could.

In marriage, it's not about avoiding cracks; it's about being willing to repair them. And often, those repaired places become the most beautiful parts of the relationship. The coffee mug may be glued back together, but its story isn't over. Every time Jasmine looks at it, she's reminded of Kyle's love, patience, and willingness to repair what was broken. And that's a story worth sharing.

Commitment, not Convience

Marriage isn't always about grand romantic gestures. It's about doing the small, unglamorous things like apologizing first, choosing kindness over being right, and sticking with your partner when life gets hard. That's the power of covenant: it calls us to love even when it's inconvenient, uncomfortable, or downright exhausting.

In Malachi 2:14-16, God says He's a witness to the marriage covenant. Why? Because He knows how hard it is to keep. But He also knows that when we honor our covenant, we reflect His love to the world.

I've done one 5k in my life and marriage is a lot like it. At the starting line, everyone's pumped. The crowd's cheering, and you're feeling good. But somewhere around the 2nd mile, the honeymoon phase was over, and I started thinking, "Why did I think this was a good idea?" That's when covenant kicks in.

Covenant says, Keep pushing, even when your knees feel like jelly. Keep going, because the finish line is worth it. And just like 5k runners, married couples don't run alone, they run with God as their coach, cheering them on every step of the way.

Marriage is Worth the Work

Kyle and Jasmine's story, reminds us that marriage isn't about avoiding cracks. It's about choosing to repair them together. God designed marriage to be a covenant because He knew we'd need something stronger than convenience to hold us together. Love is the glue, but covenant is the framework.

No matter how many mugs get broken, covenant says, "We're in this together." Because when marriage is treated as sacred, it becomes a reflection of God's unshakable love for us. And that? That's worth everything.

Chapter 2 Reflecdtion Question

In what ways does your view of marriage rflect a covenant versus a contract?

How can you practice forgiveness and restoration in your relationships, even when it's hard?

What steps can you take to ensure God is at the center of your marriage or future marriage?

CHAPTER 3

Who's the King, Who's the Queen, and Who Keeps Eating the Royal Ice Cream?

It's said that behind every great man is a great woman. But what no one tells you is that behind both of them is a pile of mismatched laundry, an overflowing calendar, and a suspiciously empty tub of ice cream someone forgot to replace. Welcome to the palace of marriage, where you and your spouse are called to rule as king and queen, not over a kingdom, but over your household, your legacy, and your lives, I guess you can call that a kingdom, but there's nothing magical about it.

Before you start thinking King and Queen means thrones and tiaras, let me set the record straight: ruling your household is less about gold crowns and more about the crowns of responsibility, collaboration, and compromise.

A Tale of Two Thrones

Sam and Monica have been married for three years, and their household is a mix of chaos and charm. Sam's the self-proclaimed King of Efficiency, known for his love of budgets, meal plans, and daily task lists. Monica, on the other hand, is the Queen of Creativity, thriving in last-minute dinner experiments, spontaneous weekend trips, and decorating the house with an ever-growing collection of holiday Pinterest fails.

One Saturday morning, Sam decided to clean the garage. To him, it was a perfectly logical way to spend the day. But when Monica walked in and saw him meticulously labeling bins, she yells, "We were supposed to have a lazy Saturday! Who cleans on a Saturday?"

Sam, looking up from his label maker, replied, A good king takes care of his kingdom. And this kingdom's garage is an embarrassment.

Monica, looking out the side of her eye, said, Your 'kingdom' doesn't even include a decent coffee maker.

The Royal Balance

Marriage isn't about two rulers fighting for the throne; it's about two rulers working together to serve the kingdom. Sam's efficiency kept the household running, but Monica's creativity brought joy and naturalness to their lives. Together, they balanced each other's strengths, just as God intended.

This dynamic mirrors God's design in Genesis 2:18, where Eve was created as a helper suitable for Adam. Helper doesn't mean subordinate; it means equal partner. Think of it like co- ruling, one has the map, and the other has the compass. Both are needed to navigate life's twists and turns.In God's design, the roles of husband and wife complement each other beautifully when done in love and respect. Here's what that looks like:

Leadership in Love

The call for a husband to lead in marriage is not a call to dominate or control; it is a call to serve with humility, love, and sacrifice. In Ephesians 5:25-28, Paul paints a powerful picture of what this leadership should look like: "Husbands, love your wives, just as Christ loved the church and gave himself up for her."

This kind of leadership mirrors Christ's relationship with

the Church, a relationship defined by selflessness, servanthood, and unconditional love. For a husband, this means putting aside ego, pride, and self-interest to prioritize the well-being of his wife and family.

A godly husband leads not by demanding submission, but by modeling servanthood. Here's what servitude as a husband looks like:

Sacrafical Love

Christ's love for the Church was sacrificial, culminating in His ultimate act of service: giving His life. A husband's leadership should reflect this sacrificial love in everyday actions, choosing to prioritize his wife's needs, dreams, and well-being above his own desires.

Example: Staying up late to help with a sick child or taking on extra responsibilities to support his wife during a challenging season.

Listening and Understanding

Leadership in love involves deeply understanding his wife's needs, fears, and aspirations. It's about actively listening, not just to respond but to empathize and support.

Example: When decisions need to be made, a godly husband ensures his wife's voice is heard and valued, fostering unity rather than imposing his will.

Leading by Example:

A husband who leads through servitude models the character he wants to see in his family. Whether it's showing patience during conflict, diligence in his work, or devotion in his faith, his actions set the tone for the household.

Example: Making time for prayer and devotion, demonstrating humility by apologizing when wrong, or treating others with kindness and respect.

Protecting and Providing:

Just as Christ protects and cares for the Church, a husband is called to provide a sense of safety and stability. This doesn't just mean financial provision, it includes emotional security, spiritual guidance, and physical protection.

Example: Ensuring his wife feels safe to express her feelings or standing by her side during difficult times with unwavering support.

Empowering and Encouraging:

Servant leadership is about lifting others up. A godly husband celebrates his wife's strengths and supports her growth, whether it's in her career, ministry, or personal passions.

Example: Actively supporting her goals, speaking life into her dreams, and being her biggest cheerleader.

It's important to clarify what servitude doesn't mean. Servanthood in marriage doesn't mean passivity, weakness, or neglecting one's role as a leader. A husband isn't called to abdicate responsibility or allow his family to lack direction.

Servitude doesn't mean becoming a doormat or enabling unhealthy dynamics. Instead, it means leading with humility, strength, and a willingness to serve without compromising integrity or biblical principles.

Wisdom Through Leadership

Oh yes, Proverbs 31 (you had to know it was coming), offers one of the most celebrated descriptions of a wise and industrious wife, a queen who embodies strength, wisdom, and purpose. Far from being a passive bystander or a mere assistant to her husband, the queen is an equal partner, a leader in her own right who brings balance, nurture, and foresight to the household.

A queen in marriage is a steward of her home, a guide for her family, and a source of inspiration. Her strength doesn't compete with her husband's leadership; it complements it. Proverbs 31:10-31 provides a vivid picture of her multifaceted role, showing us that wisdom and leadership come in many forms.

Managerial Excellence

Proverbs 31:27 says, "She watches over the affairs of her household and does not eat the bread of idleness." A queen uses her skills to manage the household with diligence and care, ensuring that the family's needs, both physical and emotional, are met.

Example: Coordinating schedules, organizing meals, or ensuring the home is a place of peace and comfort.

Financial Stewardship:

Proverbs 31:16 says, "She considers a field and buys it;

out of her earnings, she plants a vineyard." This highlights her ability to make sound financial decisions that benefit her family.

Example: Budgeting wisely, planning investments, or starting a business to contribute to the family's stability.

Providing for Needs:

Proverbs 31:20 says, "She opens her arms to the poor and extends her hands to the needy." A queen looks beyond her immediate household to serve her community, showing her compassion and generosity.

Example: Volunteering, mentoring, or finding ways to involve her family in acts of service.

Strength in Wisdom:

A queen's strength isn't in demanding recognition but in leading with grace and humility. She brings wisdom, strategy, and care to her family, ensuring that the household thrives.

Here's how her leadership manifests
A Visionary Mindset:

A queen thinks long-term, planning not just for the present but for the future. She considers how her decisions will impact her family's well-being and legacy.

Example: Preparing for her children's education, setting goals with her husband, and maintaining a vision for the family's spiritual and emotional growth.

Emotional Intelligence:

As a pillar of strength, she is often the emotional anchor for her family. She provides wisdom, comfort, and perspective during challenges.

Example: Offering counsel to her spouse during difficult decisions or helping her children navigate their emotions.

Encouragement and Influence:

Proverbs 31:26 says, "She speaks with wisdom, and faithful instruction is on her tongue." A queen uses her words to uplift, encourage, and inspire her family.

Example: Affirming her husband's efforts, guiding her children with love and wisdom, or mentoring younger women in her community.

Complentary not Competative

Leadership in marriage is a partnership, and the queen's role is to lead alongside her husband, not in opposition to him. Her strength lies in her ability to complement his leadership, bringing balance and depth to their shared vision. A queen aligns her decisions with her husband's, ensuring they are walking in agreement. Amos 3:3 reminds us, "Do two walk together unless they have agreed to do so?" This unity strengthens the family and sets an example for the next generation.

A queen doesn't diminish her husband's leadership, she amplifies it with her wisdom and support. Likewise, a godly husband honors and values his wife's contributions.

Example: Collaborating on major decisions, such as parenting strategies or financial planning, while respecting each other's insights.

The source of the queen's strength and wisdom is her relationship with God. Proverbs 31:30 says, "Charm is deceptive, and beauty is fleeting; but a woman who fears the Lord is to be praised."

Her wisdom comes from seeking God's guidance, meditating on His Word, and living out her faith in her daily actions. This spiritual foundation enables her to lead with clarity, grace, and purpose.

What the Queen Is *NOT*

It's important to note what the role of a queen *doesn't* entail:

It's not about control or overshadowing her husband's leadership.

It's not about perfection or bearing the weight of the family alone.

It's not about silencing her own dreams or ambitions to serve others.

The queen's strength lies in knowing when to lead, when to support, and when to rest. She understands that her role is both powerful and deeply interconnected with her husband's, working together to honor God.

Sam and Monica's Royal Clash

Let's go back to Sam and Monica. One evening, Monica announced she'd invited friends over for dinner, without consulting Sam. Sam panicked. "Dinner? Do we even have enough forks for that many people?"

Monica waved him off. "Relax, I'll make it work."

When the guests arrived, Monica proudly laid out a spread that looked like it had been planned for days, crafted entirely from leftovers and a box of instant rice. The compliments rolled in, with everyone raving.

Everyone except Sam, who couldn't stop glancing at the disaster zone in the kitchen. Later, as he tackled the dishes, Sam hesitated before saying, "It was great, Monica. Really. But next time, can we plan ahead? I just… I'm not great with last- minute chaos, you know?"

Monica stopped scrubbing for a moment, caught off guard. She wanted to defend herself, but as she glanced at him, she realized he wasn't criticizing, he just looked tired.

"Okay," she said softly. "But only if you promise to try my

surprise lasagna sometime. No complaints."

Sam looked at her, a small smile breaking through. "As long as I don't have to watch you cook it."

She laughed, flicking some soap suds at him. "Deal."

A Throne Room Built for Two

Picture marriage as a throne room with two chairs, one for the king and one for the queen. It's not about competition or control; it's about shared responsibility. When one person tries to claim both thrones, the room becomes unbalanced, and the kingdom suffers. But when both chairs are occupied, the household thrives. True leadership in marriage isn't measured by power but by partnership, two individuals ruling together with wisdom, humility, and love.

In 1 Peter 3:7, husbands are reminded to honor their wives as "heirs with [them] of the gracious gift of life." This verse affirms that both husband and wife are equally valuable in God's eyes, each carrying unique roles and gifts. It's not about dominance but complementarity, working together to fulfill God's purpose for their marriage.

When a king and queen rule in unity, they reflect God's design for mutual honor, shared responsibility, and sacrificial love. They don't rule for personal gain; they rule for the well-being of their kingdom. In the context of marriage, this means building a legacy for your family and future generations. This legacy isn't limited to wealth, it includes spiritual, emotional, and relational investments that impact your household and beyond.

A Kingdom Worth Building

As you consider your role, whether as a current or future king or queen, remember that ruling well requires more than power or control. It demands humility, love, and a shared vision for a legacy that lasts.

Marriage isn't just about building a household; it's about creating a kingdom worth inheriting, a place where faith, love, and mutual respect reign supreme. And when both thrones are filled with grace and purpose, the kingdom will not only stand but thrive. Whether you're the king of the chore chart or the queen of creative flair, your household is a reflection of God's design. Rule it well, and don't forget to replace the royal ice cream!

Chapter 3 Reflection Questions

How can you and your spouse (or future spouse) work together as co-rulers in your household?

In what areas do you naturally lead, and how can you use those strengths to serve your partner?

What legacy do you want to build together, and how can you start working toward it today?

CHAPTER 4

Two Are Better Than One, Unless You're Sharing a Blanket

It's said that teamwork makes the dream work, but whoever came up with that saying probably never tried to fold a fitted sheet with their spouse. Unity in marriage can feel like a beautiful waltz one minute and a three-legged race through an obstacle course the next. But here's the thing: when done right, partnership in marriage is one of the most powerful tools God gives us, not just to survive, but to thrive.

Let's start with Tom and Erica. They'd been married for six months, and one night, Tom woke up shivering. He reached over to tug on the blanket, only to find Erica had cocooned herself like a caterpillar preparing for winter.

"Seriously, Erica? Do you need the whole thing?" Tom muttered, trying to reclaim a corner of warmth.

From under the layers, Erica mumbled, "You're the one who keeps rolling away. Maybe get your own blanket and don't touch my fan."

Tom and Erica's blanket battle might seem trivial, but it highlights a deeper truth: unity doesn't happen automatically. It takes effort, compromise, and a shared commitment to working together, even when it feels easier to go solo. Proverbs 27:17 "As iron sharpens iron, so one person sharpens another."

Think of unity in marriage as something like rowing a boat. If one person rows and the other just sits there, you'll go in circles. But when both row together, in sync, you can cross oceans. And yes, that includes the ocean of clashing expectations, like who gets more blanket.

The DIY Disaster

One Saturday, Tom decided to build a bookshelf. Erica, sensing potential disaster, offered to help. "Are you sure you don't want to read the instructions?" she asked as Tom confidently spread the parts across the floor.

"Instructions are for amateurs," he replied, holding a screwdriver like a sword.

Two hours later, Erica walked in to find Tom staring at a lopsided structure that looked more like abstract art than a bookshelf. She stifled a laugh and said, "Need some help, Mr. Expert?" Together, they spent the next hour rebuilding the shelf, this time with the instructions, and by the end, it was sturdy enough to hold an actual book.

This bookshelf fiasco illustrates an important truth about unity: you can't do everything alone, nor should you try. Just as the shelf needed both of them to get it right, marriage thrives when both partners bring their unique skills, perspectives, and willingness to cooperate.

Unity doesn't mean one person takes charge while the other follows. It means learning to work together, even when you'd rather prove you're right. Philippians 2:2 says, "Make my joy complete by being like-minded, having the same love, being one in spirit and of one mind." In marriage, that often looks like choosing collaboration over competition.

The Strength of Two

Unity in marriage brings benefits that go beyond avoiding DIY disasters. Ecclesiastes 4:12 reminds us, "Though one may be overpowered, two can defend themselves. A cord of three strands is not quickly broken." The third strand is God, and when He's at the center of your marriage, your partnership becomes unshakable.

Unity in a relationship offers numerous practical benefits that strengthen the bond between partners and enhance their ability to navigate life's challenges. One significant advantage is shared strength; when one partner is weak, the other can step in to provide essential support. For instance, Tom's ability to fix things beautifully complemented Erica's knack for planning, demonstrating how their unique skills created a stronger partnership. Unity also fosters better decision-making, as two perspectives often lead to wiser choices. This was evident when Erica's suggestion to read the instructions saved them from a potential bookshelf disaster.

Beyond shared strength and decision-making, unity acts as a fortress of resilience. Facing life's storms together, whether navigating financial struggles or enduring health crises, partners who embrace unity are not just surviving; they are growing. This resilience doesn't emerge from the absence of hardship but from the conscious effort to row in tandem through life's turbulent waters. Unity, then, is the quiet, steadfast force that transforms relationships into sanctuaries and problems into purpose, enabling couples to face life's unpredictability with confidence and grace.

Ruth and Boaz

If you're looking for a biblical example of partnership done right, look no further than Ruth and Boaz. Ruth's loyalty to Naomi and her willingness to work in the fields showed her strength and commitment. Boaz, recognizing her character, stepped in as her protector and provider. Together, they created a legacy that ultimately led to the birth of King David, and, later, Jesus. Their story isn't about flashy gestures; it's about showing up for each other, day after day, and working toward a shared vision.

Unity in marriage doesn't just happen, it's a daily decision. It's deciding to share the blanket, to rebuild the bookshelf, and to row the boat together, even when it feels like you're paddling upstream. It's deciding to see your spouse as your partner, not your opponent.

Unity doesn't mean you'll always agree, but it does mean you're always on the same team. So grab the oars, share the blanket, and let God guide your marriage to something greater than either of you could achieve alone.

Chapter 4 Reflection Questions

In what areas of your life or marriage could you work on rowing together instead of separately?

How can you invite God into the areas where unity feels hard to achieve?

What's one small, practical way you can strengthen your partnership this week?

CHAPTER 5

Praying for Your Spouse, Even When You Want to Pray About Them Instead

If you've ever been married or even thought about marriage, you know there are moments when you want to pray for your spouse... and moments when you want to pray about your spouse. The difference? One keeps your marriage afloat, while the other might just land you in smite me now, Lord territory.

Marriage is a spiritual battlefield. You're not just building a life together; you're building a fortress against the world's challenges, your own insecurities, and sometimes the dishes left in the sink for three days. That's why interceding for one another is one of the most powerful acts of love you can offer your person.

The Pancake Standoff

Mia, a morning person, decided to surprise Jason with pancakes on their first Saturday as newlyweds. Jason, who needed coffee before functioning, grumbled, "Why are we eating sugar disks at 7 a.m.?"

Mia, taken aback, responded, "I thought you'd appreciate breakfast! I could've stayed in bed."

Jason sighed. "I do appreciate it... I'm just not awake enough to express it."

Mia stormed off, muttering something about "ungrateful husbands," while Jason stared at the pancakes, wondering if he'd ruined breakfast, and his marriage, in one fell swoop.

That night, Mia sat on the couch, scrolling aimlessly on her phone, fuming about Jason's comment from earlier. Meanwhile, Jason was in the bedroom, staring at the ceiling, replaying the argument in his head. Frustrated and unsure of how to fix things, they both ended up turning to prayer.

Mia muttered, "God, please help him realize how much I do for this house."

Jason sighed, "Lord, just keep her from hearing something I didn't say tomorrow. Please."

In their own corners, God quietly nudged them: You're not enemies; you're a team. Stop praying at each other, start praying for each other.

The next morning, Jason woke up early, brewed some coffee, and made pancakes, burning a couple along the way. When Mia wandered into the kitchen, still a little guarded, he held out a plate and said, "I prayed last night. And, well… consider these pancakes my burnt offering."

Mia couldn't help but smile, sitting down at the table. "I prayed too. And fine… I forgive you. But I'm praying these pancakes don't taste as bad as they look." They both laughed, realizing that sometimes, even imperfect gestures can bridge the gap.

Interceding for Your Spouse

Intercession is more than just praying for your spouse's needs, it's about standing in the gap for them spiritually, emotionally, and even physically. When you intercede, you align your heart with God's and become a vessel for His grace in your marriage. Why does this matter?

Spiritual Unity:
In Matthew 18:19-20, Jesus says, "If two of you on earth agree about anything they ask for, it will be done for them by my Father in heaven." Praying together and for each other creates spiritual unity and invites God into your marriage.

Strength in Weakness:

Marriage is not just about celebrating each other's victories, it's about standing together in the valleys of doubt, fear, and failure. In these moments, your spouse needs more than your encouragement; they need your intercession.

Galatians 6:2 calls us to "carry each other's burdens, and in this way, you will fulfill the law of Christ." This isn't just a nice sentiment; it's a divine responsibility. When your spouse is overwhelmed, discouraged, or lost, your prayers become a lifeline. Interceding for them is an act of love that goes beyond words, it's stepping into the spiritual gap and asking God to strengthen them where they feel weakest.

Carrying Their Burdens:
In the everyday reality of marriage, weakness is inevitable. Your spouse may face moments of doubting their abilities, their decisions, or even their faith. They may battle fears of failure, inadequacy, or rejection. They may carry wounds they've never

spoken aloud. In these moments, your role isn't to fix them or offer empty platitudes; it's to become their spiritual advocate.

When they don't have the strength to pray for themselves, you pray for them. When their voice is trembling with fear, your voice intercedes with faith. To carry your spouse's burdens means standing in the spiritual trenches and saying, You're not in this alone. I'll fight for you, with you, and beside you.

Power of Intercesion

Interceding for your spouse is not just about asking God to take away their struggles. It's about partnering with God in their transformation. It's praying:

Lord, remind them of who You've called them to be,
Strengthen their heart when it feels weak and weary.
Help me be the partner they need in this season.

In doing so, you're not only lifting your spouse's burdens to God, you're also reminding them of the truth: that they are deeply loved, not only by you but by a God who sees them fully and completely.

Strength in Weakness

It's often in our most vulnerable moments that God's power is made perfect. 2 Corinthians 12:9 declares, "My grace is sufficient for you, for my power is made perfect in weakness." When you intercede for your spouse, you're not asking God to erase their struggles but to reveal His strength through them. You're praying that they would experience His grace, His wisdom, and His peace in a way they never have before. This is the beauty of marriage, God uses your love, patience, and faithfulness to reflect His own love for your spouse.

When you make intercession a regular part of your marriage, you're building a legacy of spiritual strength. You're teaching your children, friends, and community what it means to love deeply, not just in word but in action.

In a world that often says, Handle it yourself, intercession reminds us that we were never meant to carry our burdens alone. Praying for your spouse is a way to show them, When you feel like you're falling, I'm here to hold you up. When you feel like giving up, I'll remind you of why you started. And when you feel unseen, I'll remind you that God is always watching over you.

Marriage is a partnership not just in joy but in struggle. In moments of weakness, the greatest gift you can give your spouse is the strength of your prayers. Interceding for them is not just an act of love, it's a reminder of the divine truth: In Christ, weakness is never the end of the story. It's the place where His power begins.

So the next time your spouse falters, don't just stand by, stand in. Pray boldly. Pray faithfully. And in doing so, remind them that together, with God, you are unshakable.

Protecting Your Marriage

In Ephesians 6:12, Paul reminds us that our battles are not against flesh and blood but against spiritual forces. Praying for your spouse helps safeguard your marriage against unseen attacks.

Fast forward a year, and Jason and Mia had made it a habit to pray for each other regularly. This practice had become a cornerstone of their marriage, one they leaned on in moments of peace and in moments of tension. But like all habits, it wasn't always easy to live out.

One evening, after a particularly grueling week at work, Jason snapped at Mia over something trivial, whether the dishwasher was loaded wrong or who left the light on didn't matter. What mattered was the sting of his words. Mia, tired and already running low on patience, retreated to the bedroom, shutting the door a little louder than she intended. Sitting on the edge of the bed, she felt the familiar swell of frustration and hurt.

In that moment, Mia couldn't help but think of the hippo and the bird. Jason, right now, was the hippo, massive, strong, and trudging through life's muddy waters, leaving ripples and chaos in his wake without even noticing.

Mia, by contrast, felt like the bird perched on the hippo's back. It wasn't her job to control the hippo or fix his path, that was up to him. But it was her role to bring perspective and balance, even when his movements were unpredictable and overwhelming.

Still, the bird has its limits. She thought, How many times

do I have to hover above this mess? But the hippo and the bird don't thrive in opposition, they work best in partnership. The bird benefits from the hippo's strength, and the hippo relies on the bird's vision.

Instead of letting her frustration take over, Mia closed her eyes and prayed:

Lord, I'm tired. Help me love Jason even when he's acting like... well, a hippo. Give him peace in his stress, and help me be patient enough to meet him where he is.

Meanwhile, in the living room, Jason sat slumped on the couch, head in his hands. He felt like he was sinking, overwhelmed by work, stress, and the realization that he'd hurt Mia again. He was the hippo. Strong, sure, but sometimes oblivious to the impact of his weight on the people around him.

Jason sighed and muttered a prayer of his own:

God, I don't know what I'm doing. Help me to stop charging ahead without thinking, and help me make things right with my bird.

As Mia was curled up with her phone, still feeling hurt but calmer after her prayer. Jason stood by the door for a moment, his usual confidence replaced with humility.

"I apologize," he said quietly, his voice carrying the weight of both regret and vulnerability. "I've been overwhelmed, and I took it out on you. That wasn't fair."

Mia looked up, her expression softening. "I know," she said.

Jason chuckled as he sat on the edge of the bed beside her. "You're better at this than I am."

Mia smirked, leaning into him. "I'm not better, I just decided to stop being the bird that flies off in frustration and let God handle things for once."

The Power of Partnership

The same hippo and bird from Chapter 1 are a reminder of how different partners can be, yet how much they depend on each other to thrive. Remember, the hippo brings strength, endurance, and the ability to wade through the messiest waters. The bird brings perspective, alertness, and the ability to see the bigger picture.

While the hippo and the bird demonstrate how our differences can complement one another, each role comes with its own potential pitfalls. Recognizing these negatives helps partners grow in self-awareness and find balance in your relationship.

When stress and emotions run high, both can forget their roles. The hippo may stomp through the mud without thinking, and the bird may fly off in exaperation. The lesson Jason and Mia learned that night is simple but profound: their differences aren't weaknesses, they're the key to their partnership.

The Negatives of Being a Hippo

Oblivious to the Impact of Their Actions:

Hippos, in their single-minded focus or stress, can trample over their partner's feelings without realizing it. Their strength can become a burden when not handled with care.

Example: A stressed partner might brush off their spouse's concerns, dismissing them as insignificant in the face of bigger problems.

Hippos are creatures of habit. In marriage, this can translate to stubbornness or reluctance to adapt, even when change is needed for the relationship to thrive.

Example: Preferring their routine over compromising on new ways to connect or support their spouse.

Emotional Suppression:

The hippo's strength can lead to bottling up emotions to appear unshakable. This can create distance, as vulnerability is essential to intimacy.

Example: Saying, "I'm fine," when stressed instead of opening up, leaving your partner feeling shut out.

Overbearing Presence:

In conflict or stress, the hippo's natural tendency to charge through can dominate conversations or situations, leaving their partner feeling unheard or overwhelmed.
Example: Insisting their way is the only way forward in a disagreement.

The Negatives of Being a Bird

Overly Reactive:

Birds, with their quick reflexes, can be overly sensitive or reactive to the hippo's movements. This can lead to overanalyzing or jumping to conclusions.

Example: Assuming the hippo's stress or withdrawal is a personal slight rather than a reflection of their own struggles.

Tendency to Flee:

Birds have the ability to fly away when things get tough, which in marriage can translate to avoidance or disengagement instead of working through issues.

Example: Leaving the room during an argument or emotionally withdrawing instead of addressing the conflict.

To bring balance, birds may take on too much responsibility, trying to fix the relationship or manage their partner's emotions. This can lead to burnout or resentment.

Example: Always being the one to apologize or smooth things over, even when it's not your fault.

Lack of Grounding:

While the bird's perspective is valuable, they can sometimes lack grounding, focusing on hypothetical or future concerns instead of dealing with the present reality.

Example: Worrying excessively about long-term problems while neglecting immediate needs in the relationship.

When the Negatives Colliade

If the hippo's and bird's flaws are left unchecked, their differences can create tension instead of harmony. The Hippo Overwhelms; the Bird Withdraws. The hippo's emotional weight and lack of awareness can push the bird to retreat, leaving both feeling isolated and misunderstood. The hippo feels abandoned, and the bird feels unseen.

The bird overcompensates; the hippo resists. The bird's attempt to fix everything can make the hippo feel micromanaged, leading to stubbornness and further distance.

Then the bird feels overburdened, and the hippo feels criticized.

When both avoid vulnerability, the hippo will suppress emotions, and the bird will avoid confrontation, creating a communication gap where issues fester instead of being resolved, and resentment will build as neither feels truly understood or supported.

How to Overcome

For the Hippo:

Cultivate Self-Awareness: Regularly check in with your partner to understand how your actions or stress may be affecting them.

Practice Vulnerability: Open up about your struggles instead of charging through them alone.

Be Intentional: Slow down and make space for your partner's needs and concerns.

For the Bird:

Stay Grounded: Focus on what's happening in the present instead of flying off into hypotheticals.

Address Issues Directly: Resist the urge to flee or avoid conflict; lean into difficult conversations with grace.

Share the Load: Recognize that you're not responsible for

fixing everything, allow your partner to step up, even if it takes time.

Communicate Openly: Share your needs and frustrations without assuming the worst about each other.

Celebrate Differences: Remember that your unique strengths are meant to complement, not compete.

Pray Together: Inviting God into your relationship can help bridge the gap between your differences, reminding you that you're a team, not opponents.

Embracing Growth Together

The negatives of being a hippo or bird don't define the relationship, they're simply areas for growth. When both partners recognize their tendencies and commit to working through them, their differences can become their greatest strengths.

In every marriage, there will be moments when one partner feels like the hippo and the other feels like the bird. Recognizing these patterns helps avoid unnecessary conflict.

Just as the hippo and bird thrive together, so do you and your spouse. Celebrate what each of you brings to the relationship, even when those differences feel frustrating at that moment. Humility from the hippo and grace from the bird can break the cycle of conflict and create space for healing and connection.

The hippo and the bird aren't perfect, but they're better together. And so are Jason and Mia, and so are you and your spouse. Together, with humility, grace, and a little divine help, you can navigate the muddy waters of life and build a partnership that thrives.

Imagine a game of tug-of-war. If both people pull against each other, nothing moves—or worse, someone gets hurt. But what if you dropped the rope and started pulling in the same direction? That's what prayer does. It takes the tension and redirects it toward God, aligning both of you with His purpose.

In Colossians 3:13, Paul writes, "Bear with each other and forgive one another if any of you has a grievance against someone. Forgive as the Lord forgave you." Interceding for your spouse helps you move from grievance to grace, from frustration to forgiveness.

The beauty of interceding for your spouse is that it doesn't just impact your marriage—it impacts your family, your community, and future generations. Jason and Mia learned that prayer wasn't just a survival tool; it was a legacy-building practice.

Interceding for your spouse isn't just about changing their heart—it's about letting God change yours too. So the next time she leaves the dishes in the sink or he burns the pancakes, pause, pray, and let God do the heavy lifting. After all, marriage isn't just about surviving each other; it's about thriving together in Him.

Chapter 5 Reflection Questions

What's one area where your spouse (or future spouse) could use prayer right now?

How can you create a habit of praying for your spouse daily?

When was the last time you asked God to help you see your spouse through His eyes?

CHAPTER 6

It's Not Your Money or My Money, It's God's Money.

If you want to test the strength of a marriage, hand the couple a joint checking account and watch what happens.

Money isn't just paper and numbers; it's a magnifying glass, exposing every difference in priorities, habits, and hidden Amazon purchases (yes, we see those packages). But here's the good news, when handled with unity, money doesn't have to divide, it can multiply blessings, build legacies, and bring freedom.

The Great Budget Debate

Alicia and Marcus are navigating the thrilling yet terrifying world of shared finances. Alicia, the spender, loved treating herself to coffee shop lattes and spontaneous shopping trips.
Marcus, the investor, could stretch a dollar so far it squealed.

One Saturday morning, Marcus sat down. "We need to talk about the budget," he said. Alicia, sipping a $9 Venti Caramel Ribbon Crunch Frappuccino, rolled her eyes. "You mean your budget?"

Marcus sighed. "Our budget. We're a team now. And we can't spend money we don't have."

Alicia smirked. "Fine. But don't expect me to eat rice and beans for the next 30 years just to save $1.50 on milk."

Money in marriage is often described as a source of conflict, but it doesn't have to be. Instead, think of it as a treasure chest, a place where your shared resources, dreams, and priorities are stored. This chest has the potential to bless your household abundantly, but only if it's managed with trust, communication, and wisdom.

If one partner holds the key, making all the decisions or controlling the finances, the other is left feeling powerless and excluded. On the flip side, if one partner recklessly digs through the chest without accountability, spending without regard for their spouse's input, the chest will quickly empty, leaving both partners resentful and burdened.

The real power of the treasure chest is unlocked when both partners share responsibility for it. This doesn't necessarily mean splitting every financial task, but it does mean cultivating openness, trust, and mutual respect in how money is handled. Stewarding your finances wisely as a team transforms the treasure chest from a potential source of bitterness into a wellspring of blessings for your marriage, your family, and even your future generations.

In Matthew 6:21, Jesus said,

For where your treasure is, there your heart will be also.

Marriage invites you to put your treasure, and your heart into a shared vision. It's not about ownership; it's about stewardship.

What is the Key?

The treasure chest thrives on honesty. Both partners need to know what's in the chest, your income, expenses, savings, and goals. Financial secrets or surprises can feel like betrayal, eroding trust and unity.

Practical Tip: Schedule regular "money dates" to review your finances together, celebrate progress, and adjust plans as needed.

Define Your Shared Values

Money isn't just about numbers, it's about what those numbers represent, security, freedom, generosity, or opportunity. Couples need to align their values to ensure that spending and saving reflect their shared priorities.

Example: If one partner values saving for a home while the other prioritizes experiences like travel, compromise is key to finding balance.

If one partner insists on holding the key, controlling all decisions, it creates an imbalance of power. The other partner may feel unheard or undervalued, which can lead to resentment or reckless spending as an act of rebellion.

Practical Tip: Divide financial responsibilities based on strengths but ensure both partners have a voice in major decisions.

Stewardship vs. Ownership

In marriage, money isn't about ownership, it's about stewardship. As a couple, you're called to steward your finances in a way that honors God and strengthens your family. This means shifting the mindset from my money or your money to our money.

Proverbs 3:9 reminds us to *Honor the Lord with your wealth.* Stewardship starts with recognizing that the treasure in your chest is a gift from God, entrusted to you for wise management. Whether you're in a season of abundance or scarcity, how you steward your resources reflects your values, priorities, and commitment to each other.

When both partners work together to manage the treasure chest, it becomes more than just a source of provision; it becomes a source of blessing.

Shared financial management reduces tension and prevents misunderstandings, creating harmony in the household.

Working together allows you to set boundaries on spending, save for future goals, and avoid unnecessary debt.

A united approach to money creates opportunities to give, bless others, and invest in causes that align with your shared values.

Wise stewardship leaves an inheritance, not just financially, but in the lessons you model for your children about teamwork and trust.

Sharing the Treasure Chest

Create a Joint Budget:

Outline your income, expenses, and goals together. A budget isn't restrictive—it's freeing, giving you both clarity and control over your finances.

Celebrate Small Wins:

Whether it's paying off a credit card, saving for a vacation, or sticking to your grocery budget, celebrate your progress as a team. These moments build unity and reinforce shared goals.

Practice Generosity Together:

Use your treasure chest to bless others. Agree on causes or people you'd like to support, and make giving a shared joy in your marriage.

Plan for the Future:

Discuss long-term goals like retirement, saving for children's education, or purchasing a home. Working toward these milestones together deepens your sense of partnership.

Avoiding the Pitfalls

Even the strongest treasure chest can weaken if it's mishandled:

Neglect:

Ignoring financial issues, like mounting debt or

unchecked spending, can lead to crisis.

Assumptions:

Assuming your partner agrees with your financial decisions without discussing them can breed conflict.

Blame:

Pointing fingers during financial struggles only divides the partnership. Instead, tackle challenges as a team.

Building a Blessing, not a Burden

The treasure chest in marriage is not just a container for dollars and cents; it's a vessel for shared dreams, a tool for building a future, and a symbol of your commitment to each other. When stewarded wisely, your treasure chest becomes a reflection of God's provision and your partnership. It's no longer a source of division but a cornerstone of your legacy, a blessing that will impact not just your marriage but all who come across you.

God's Word is full of wisdom on handling money, and it all comes down to this: it's not ours to begin with. Psalm 24:1 reminds us, *The earth is the Lord's, and everything in it.* When we view our finances as God's resources, we shift from competing over money to collaborating as stewards. Key Principles for Financial Freedom:

Unity Over Independence
Planning Over Impulse
Generosity Over Greed
The Joint Account Agreement

After several months of budget battles, Alicia and Marcus had a breakthrough. Instead of focusing on what they couldn't do, they started dreaming about what they could do together. Marcus got his spreadsheets, and Alicia got a "fun money" category for her lattes. They started saving for a home and giving more to their church. Each month, they asked God for wisdom and direction. It wasn't perfect, but it was progress. And for the first time, they felt like partners, not opponents.

The Three Servants

Jesus told a parable in Matthew 25:14-30 about a master who gave three servants bags of gold to steward while he was away. Two of the servants invested wisely and doubled their money, while the third buried his in fear and laziness. When the master returned, he rewarded the faithful servants and rebuked the one who wasted his resources.

In marriage, you and your spouse are like those servants. God has entrusted you with resources, not just money, but time, energy, and talents, and God expects you to use them wisely.

Financial freedom isn't about hoarding wealth;
it's about multiplying God's blessings.

A year into their new system, Alicia and Marcus faced an unexpected challenge: their car broke down, and the repair bill was $800. In the past, this would've been a crisis. But thanks to their budget and emergency fund, they handled it without stress.

That night, as they sat down to dinner, Alicia raised her glass of sparkling water. "Here's to not panicking about the car." Marcus grinned. "Here's to teamwork, and maybe fewer lattes."

Alicia and Marcus learned that financial freedom isn't just about dollars and cents, it's about aligning their hearts and resources with God's purpose. By working together, they moved from stress to stewardship, from conflict to collaboration. In the process, they discovered that money, when handled wisely, can be a tool for building the kind of marriage—and legacy—that glorifies God.

And remember, financial freedom isn't about having more money—it's about managing what you have with wisdom, unity, and a shared vision. So grab the budget, say a prayer, and start building your treasure chest—together.

Chapter 6 Reflection Questions

What's one financial habit you or your spouse could improve to create unity in your marriage?

How can you shift your perspective from ownership to stewardship when it comes to money?

What financial goals could you set as a couple to honor God and build a legacy?

CHAPTER 7

Can You Hear Me Now?

Marriage is often described as a journey. There are seasons when you're strolling hand-in-hand through a scenic path, feeling God's presence every step of the way. And then there are seasons when the path feels uphill, the scenery is more wilderness than garden, and God's voice seems as silent as a phone in airplane mode. If you've ever felt spiritually disconnected in your marriage—whether from your spouse, God, or both—you're not alone.

The Silent Treatment

Let me tell you about Elena and Rob. Early in their marriage, Elena prided herself on being the spiritual leader of the household. She was up at dawn for prayer and Bible study, constantly sharing devotionals with Rob, and volunteering at church. Rob, however, was in a season of spiritual burnout. He was barely making it through the workweek and felt guilty about not being spiritual enough.

One evening, after Elena suggested they pray together for the third time that week, Rob snapped. "Why do you always push this on me? Maybe I don't feel like praying right now!" Elena was stunned. She hadn't realized that her well-meaning encouragement had felt like pressure to Rob. That night, as she lay in bed, Elena whispered a frustrated prayer: "Lord, I'm trying my best here. Why does it feel like I'm the only one holding this marriage together?"

Marriage is your desert. Sometimes, one partner is parched and weary while the other is closer to the oasis. The key is to recognize that you're still walking together, even if you're at different stages. When God feels distant, it's not a sign to stop walking, it's a call to lean on each other and press forward.

In Psalm 63:1, David writes, *You, God, are my God, earnestly I seek you; I thirst for you, my whole being longs for you, in a dry and parched land where there is no water.* Even spiritual dryness can become an opportunity for growth, if you face it together.

Spiritual disconnection in marriage can happen for many reasons. Thinking your spouse should be your constant source of spiritual strength can lead to frustration. Only God can fill that role. Busyness, stress, and fatigue can make it hard to prioritize spiritual connection. Emotional distance from your spouse often mirrors spiritual distance from God. Spiritual intimacy, like physical intimacy, requires effort and attention.

The Parking Lot

After yet another argument over Rob's lack of spiritual involvement, Elena felt a familiar frustration creeping in. She wanted him to lead their family in faith, but every time she brought it up, the conversation turned into a battle. That night, instead of rehashing her frustrations, Elena made a quiet decision, she was going to stop pressuring Rob and start praying for him.

She pulled out a stack of Post-It notes, wrote a simple prayer on the first one, "Lord, guide Rob's heart and bring us closer to You." and tucked it inside her Bible. Every time she felt the urge to push Rob or bring up his lack of engagement, she reached for another Post-It and wrote a prayer instead. Her stack grew, creating a kind of parking lot for her hopes, frustrations, and trust in God's ability to work in Rob's heart.

Weeks later, during breakfast, Rob noticed the stack of colorful Post-Its tucked near Elena's Bible. He held one up and read it aloud:

"Lord, help Rob find peace and purpose in You."

"What's this?" he asked, his voice a mix of curiosity and confusion.

"They're my prayers for you," Elena said gently. "I decided to talk to God about you instead of trying to change you."

Rob was stunned. For the first time, he didn't feel like a project Elena was trying to fix or a box she needed him to check. Instead, he felt genuinely seen, not for who she wanted him to be, but for who he was right now. He realized her prayers weren't about controlling him, they were about trusting God to do what only He could.

The Power of the Parking Lot

The Post-It parking lot became a silent yet powerful symbol of surrender. For Elena, it was a way to channel her concerns into prayer instead of nagging or pushing Rob, which often left both of them feeling defensive. It was a reminder that God's timing, not hers, would lead to transformation. For Rob, the stack of Post-Its was a visual representation of Elena's faith —not in him, but in God's ability to guide him. It softened his resistance, showing him that her desire for him to grow spiritually wasn't about criticism but about love and hope for their family.

That evening, Rob approached Elena with a vulnerability she hadn't seen in months. "You wanna pray tonight?" he asked quietly. It wasn't an elaborate gesture, but for them, it was a monumental step.

For Elena the Post-Its became a tangible expression of her prayers, reminding her daily to trust God with her concerns instead of taking matters into her own hands. Writing down her prayers helped her release her need for immediate change and focus on interceding for Rob in love, not frustration. Instead of pushing Rob with her own agenda, Elena invited God to work in both their hearts, creating space for transformation to happen naturally. For Rob, seeing the prayers helped him realize Elena wasn't trying to manipulate him but was genuinely rooting for his growth in faith.

Over time, the Post-It parking lot didn't just change Rob — it changed Elena too. It taught her patience, reminded her of God's sovereignty, and helped her see Rob not as a project but as her partner. For Rob, the prayers became a bridge between their spiritual disconnect and a deeper connection with both God and Elena.

Their marriage began to shift, not because of one big conversation or dramatic change, but because Elena chose to trust the process and pray persistently. The Post-It notes became more than just scraps of paper; they became symbols of a marriage rooted in grace, love, and faith.

The story of Elena and Rob reminds us that transformation in marriage isn't about forcing change, it's about trusting God to lead the process. The Post-It parking lot is a practical way to surrender your worries and channel them into prayer, creating space for God to work in His timing.

And as Rob and Elena discovered, when one partner chooses faith over frustration, it often inspires the other to take the first step toward change. Small acts of surrender can lead to big moments of connection, making the treasure of prayer one of the greatest tools in a thriving marriage.

Think of your marriage like a tree. One partner might be thriving, reaching toward the sun, while the other is struggling in the shade. Instead of judging the weaker tree, the stronger one can act as a gardener, nurturing, watering, and patiently waiting for new growth.

In John 15:5, Jesus says, *I am the vine; you are the branches. If you remain in me and I in you, you will bear much fruit; apart from me you can do nothing.* A spiritually strong marriage relies on both partners remaining connected to Christ, even when one feels distant.

Reconnecting Spiritually

Pray Individually (and Together):

Start with small, manageable steps—like praying over meals or sharing a Scripture verse.

Create Space for Vulnerability:

Ask open-ended questions about your spouse's spiritual needs without judgment.

Focus on Gratitude:

Thank God for your spouse, even during hard seasons. Gratitude shifts your perspective and invites God's presence. Join a couples' Bible study, small group, or serve together at church to foster spiritual connection.

Be Patient:

Spiritual growth doesn't happen overnight. Trust God to work in His timing.

Even when God feels distant, He is still working behind the scenes to strengthen your marriage. Sometimes, He uses the dry seasons to teach us humility, dependence, and perseverance. So keep walking, keep praying, and trust that the desert will lead to the oasis.

Chapter 7 Reflection Questions

When have you felt spiritually distant in your marriage? How did you handle it?

What steps can you take to reconnect with your spouse and with God?

How can you support your spouse during their seasons of spiritual dryness?

CHAPTER 8
No Respect, No Rhythm

It's Valentine's Day. Jamie, ever the romantic, surprises his wife, Nicole, with roses, chocolates, and a handwritten note that says, "You're my everything." He's grinning, expecting a hug or maybe even a happy tear. Instead, Nicole looks up from the laundry pile and says, "This is sweet, but what I really wanted was for you to fix the dishwasher."

Jamie is dumbfounded. He mutters, "I pour my heart out, and all you care about is the dishwasher?" Nicole fires back, "And I've been pouring my heart out asking you to fix it for three weeks!"

Cue awkward silence.

Jamie and Nicole's story is a classic example of mismatched expectations. Jamie was expressing love, but Nicole was craving respect. Love and respect are the two left and right feet of a marriage. Without them, you're not dancing
—you're stumbling.

Love and respect are foundational rhythms of a thriving marriage—like the left and right feet in a dance. When both are present, the relationship moves gracefully, creating harmony and connection. But when one or both are missing, it's not a dance anymore—it's a stumble, a clumsy attempt to move forward without balance or coordination.

Picture this, A couple trying to waltz, but one partner is stepping on toes while the other stands still, unsure of what to do next. That's what marriage feels like without love and respect. The rhythm is off, the connection is strained, and instead of moving as a team, you're stepping on each other's efforts.

Love is the tender care, the selfless giving, and the emotional safety that every spouse craves. It's the embrace after an argument, the small acts of kindness, and the willingness to put the other person's needs ahead of your own.

Respect is the acknowledgment of worth, the valuing of each other's opinions, and the appreciation of each other's efforts. It's listening without dismissing, affirming without controlling and encouraging without belittling. Together, they create the rhythm that keeps the marriage moving forward. Without love, respect feels cold and transactional. Without respect, love feels shallow and condescending.

When one Foot is Missing

Without Love:

A spouse who feels respected but not loved often experiences emotional emptiness. They may feel like a coworker or roommate rather than a cherished partner.

Example: You might say, "I appreciate everything you do," but if you're not showing affection, your spouse may still feel distant.

Without Respect:

A spouse who feels loved but not respected often experiences frustration and disconnection. They may feel like their contributions are undervalued or that their voice doesn't matter.

Example: You might say, "I love you so much," but if you dismiss their ideas or make decisions without consulting them, they'll feel ignored.

In both cases, the marriage stumbles. One partner feels overlooked, the other feels misunderstood, and the connection weakens over time. To keep the rhythm of your marriage, both partners must actively practice love and respect, stepping in sync to create harmony:

Step 1: Lead with Love

Love isn't just a feeling; it's an action. Show your spouse they are cherished through consistent, intentional gestures. This could be as simple as making their favorite coffee, writing a thoughtful note, or offering a listening ear when they've had a tough day.

Step 2: Show Respect Daily

Respect is demonstrated in how you speak, listen, and respond to your spouse. Avoid sarcasm or dismissive comments. Instead, affirm their value by showing genuine interest in their thoughts, dreams, and struggles.

Step 3: Stay in Sync

Just as dancing requires communication, so does maintaining love and respect. Ask for feedback, apologize when you stumble, and adjust and keep moving together.

Step 4: Recognize the Needs

Ephesians 5:33 says, *Each one of you must love his wife as he loves himself, and the wife must respect her husband.* While both love and respect are essential for both partners, men often crave respect as their foundation, while women often feel secure in love. Understanding this can help you meet each other's unique needs.

The Beauty of the Dance

When love and respect are in balance, marriage transforms into a beautiful dance. Each partner moves with confidence, supporting and uplifting the other. Missteps are inevitable, but they're quickly corrected because the foundation of the relationship is strong.

Imagine a couple gliding across the dance floor—each step fluid, each movement intentional. That's what love and respect do for a marriage. They take the mundane rhythms of everyday life and turn them into something extraordinary.

Without love and respect, you're stumbling, stepping on

toes, and wondering why the connection feels off. But when both are present, you're not just moving—you're dancing, creating a partnership that reflects grace, harmony, and joy.

Are you dancing with your spouse, or are you stumbling through the steps? If you're stumbling, it's never too late to find the rhythm again. Love and respect are always waiting for you to take the next step—together.

The Spilled Coffee

Imagine a husband and wife walking together, each carrying a cup of coffee. The husband accidentally bumps into his wife, spilling her coffee everywhere. Instead of apologizing, he says, "Well, if you didn't fill it so high, this wouldn't have happened." Hurt, she snaps back, "If you'd watch where you were going, I wouldn't have spilled it!"

This coffee clash is how love and respect operate. Love says, "I'm sorry I bumped you—how can I make it right?" Respect says, "I'll give you space to carry your coffee your way." When both are present, even the spills of life can be managed with grace. So how do I recognize Loving vs Respecting?

Different Needs for Different Tanks

There are two gas tanks, one for love and one for respect.

Both tanks are essential to keep the relationship running smoothly. If either runs empty, the journey together becomes strained, and the relationship can stall. But here's the catch: these tanks don't fill themselves. It takes intentionality, effort, and consistency to keep both tanks full.

Just as cars run on different types of gas—regular, premium, or diesel—love and respect are like two unique fuels designed to meet your partner's deepest emotional needs.

The Love Tank:

The love tank requires emotional connection and affection. It's filled through gestures that show care, intimacy, and appreciation.

For some, this looks like physical touch, heartfelt conversations, or words of affirmation. For others, it's acts of service, like making a favorite meal or helping with a task that makes their day easier.

The Respect Tank:

The respect tank thrives on acknowledgment and appreciation for contributions. It's filled by valuing your partner's efforts, recognizing their strengths, and treating them as an equal in the relationship.

This might mean expressing gratitude for the way they provide for the family, supporting their dreams, or respecting their opinions during decisions.

Both tanks are crucial for everyone, it's common for men to primarily draw energy from their respect tank and women from their love tank.

Nicole had been frustrated with the dishwasher for weeks. She'd mentioned it to Jamie, but he hadn't gotten around to fixing it. When Jamie finally tackled the project, taking the time to repair it himself, Nicole felt respected. It wasn't just about the dishwasher—it was about Jamie valuing her frustrations and stepping up to take action. That act filled her respect tank.

Meanwhile, Jamie had been feeling disconnected after a tough week at work.

One evening, Nicole surprised him by cooking his favorite meal—something small, but deeply personal. To Jamie, this wasn't just dinner; it was a reminder that Nicole cared enough to pay attention to his preferences and go out of her way to bring him comfort. That simple act topped off his love tank.

Notice that these gestures weren't grand or expensive. They were intentional, meeting each other's needs in a way that spoke directly to their hearts.

Identify Each Other's Fuel Type

Just like you wouldn't put diesel in a car that requires premium, it's important to understand what fuels your partner. Take the time to learn what makes them feel most loved and respected.

Make Regular Fill-Ups:

Don't wait for the tank to run empty. Be proactive in meeting each other's needs through small, consistent gestures. A simple "thank you" for something your partner did or a spontaneous hug can go a long way.

Communicate When You're Running Low:

Don't let resentment build. If you feel like your tank is running low, express your needs kindly and clearly. For example, Nicole could say, "I really appreciate everything you've been doing, but I'd love for us to spend some more quality time together."

Balance Is Key:

Focus on filling both tanks equally. Overfilling one while neglecting the other can leave your marriage lopsided. Make sure love and respect flow freely in both directions.

When both tanks are full, marriage moves effortlessly, like a well-maintained car cruising down the road. The love tank keeps the relationship warm, nurturing emotional intimacy, while the respect tank keeps it steady, fostering trust and mutual appreciation.

And just like a car can travel farther on a full tank, a marriage fueled by consistent love and respect is equipped to handle the long haul—the challenges, changes, and triumphs of life. After all, marriage isn't a sprint—it's a journey. And with both tanks full, you can enjoy the ride together and go farther.

Love and respect aren't a one-time event—they're a daily dance. Sometimes, you'll step on each other's toes, but as long as you keep moving together, you'll find your rhythm. So grab your partner, fix the dishwasher, and start dancing like no one's watching.

Chapter 8 Reflection Questions

In what ways do you naturally show love or respect to your spouse?

Where could you improve in meeting your spouse's needs for love or respect?

How can you invite God to help you break cycles of misunderstanding in your marriage?

CHAPTER 9
Building a Life Without Losing Yourself

Marriage is a duet: two voices blending to create a harmony that neither could achieve alone. It's beautiful when the voices are in sync—but what happens when one partner wants to sing jazz while the other prefers the structure of classical music? What happens when your dreams take you in seemingly opposite directions?

Travel Dreamer vs. Homebody

Emma has always dreamed of exploring the world, backpacking across Europe, immersing herself in different cultures, and chasing new adventures at every turn. She thrives on the excitement of new places, the thrill of not knowing what's around the next corner, and the chance to grow through experience.

On the other hand, her husband, Adam, finds comfort in stability. He loves their home, the familiarity of their community, and the predictability of a well-set routine. His idea of a perfect weekend is staying home, working on house projects, and enjoying a quiet evening in with Emma.

It's as if Emma wants to sing a lively jazz tune, full of improvisation and spontaneity, while Adam prefers the rich, steady rhythms of a classical symphony. Neither of them is wrong, they're simply different. And these differences, while challenging, can create the opportunity to build a duet that's richer and more nuanced than either of them could achieve alone.

The Song Your Partner Wants to Sing

Emma and Adam took the time to understand why their dreams mattered to each of them. For Emma, travel wasn't just about seeing new places; it was about feeling alive, gaining new perspectives, and growing as a person. For Adam, stability wasn't about staying put—it was about feeling secure, building a nest they could always come back to, and enjoying the sense of home.

Instead of trying to force each other into their own rhythm, they found a middle ground. They planned one big trip each year—a chance for Emma to embrace adventure while Adam prepared himself for the experience, knowing he could always come back to the comfort of their home. And in between trips, they dedicated weekends to home-based activities Adam loved, gardening, fixing up their home, and hosting dinner with friends.

Rather than seeing their differences as an obstacle, Emma and Adam began celebrating each other's passions. Emma would get excited about home projects, putting her creativity into redecorating a room with Adam. Adam, in turn, embraced Emma's love for travel, even researching new places they could visit on YouTube and surprising her with a map to mark their future adventures.

The Opportunity for Growth

Balancing personal purpose with shared partnership can feel like juggling flaming torches while riding a unicycle, while impressive, it takes practice, patience, and a willingness to adapt. But these moments of difference, rather than tearing the relationship apart, became the key to Emma and Adam's growth:

For Emma, as a bird, learning to embrace stability helped her appreciate the beauty of routine and grounded her adventurous spirit. She found joy in the quiet moments at home and learned that sometimes, stability offers its own kind of adventure, one rooted in deep connection and comfort.

For Adam, the hippo, stepping out of his comfort zone and embracing travel taught him to let go of control, enjoy spontaneity, and see the world through a broader lens. He learned that adventure wasn't something to fear, but a way to grow alongside Emma, discovering new aspects of life together.

God didn't design marriage to stifle individuality, He designed it to amplify your purpose. In Genesis 2:18, God calls Eve a helper suitable for Adam. The Hebrew word for helper ezer doesn't mean subordinate; it means partner, ally, and supporter. Together, Adam and Eve were tasked with stewarding creation, a shared mission that required both of their strengths. Each spouse has a God-given purpose. Ignoring one partner's calling in favor of the other creates resentment.

Instead, celebrate and support each other's strengths. While individual dreams are important, a shared vision keeps the marriage grounded. How can your individual purposes complement the life you're building together?

Trust God's Timing

Ecclesiastes 3:1 reminds us, *There is a time for everything, and a season for every activity under the heavens.* Not every dream needs to be pursued at the same time.

Acknowledge and celebrate each other's progress, no matter how small. Success feels sweeter when it's shared.

When the Bird and Hippo Clash

Just as Emma and Adam initially struggled to harmonize their dreams of travel and stability, the bird and the hippo can find their differences frustrating. Their duet wasn't about one changing their tune to match the other, it was about creating a new song altogether. A piece that included adventure and stability, improvisation and structure, jazz and classical.

In marriage, harmony isn't about singing the same notes all the time. It's about listening to each other, blending your unique melodies, and finding a way to make the differences add depth rather than dissonance.

The key is understanding that different dreams don't mean incompatible dreams. Emma and Adam found that by blending their songs—by singing each other's tunes at times, and by finding moments to create new music—they were able to grow individually and as a couple.

The beauty of a duet lies not in uniformity, but in the richness of two voices, each distinct, coming together to create something unique and beautiful. Marriage is the same: when you embrace each other's rhythms, even if they're different, you create a harmony that is powerful and unforgettable.

New Duets in Action

In Everyday Life:

The bird might propose a spontaneous weekend getaway, while the hippo suggests setting a budget and planning the logistics. Instead of clashing, they find a way to balance freedom and structure, making the getaway both exciting and feasible.

In Big Decisions:

The bird dreams of starting a business, while the hippo values financial stability. They could work together by creating a detailed business plan that satisfies the hippo's need for security while honoring the bird's desire for freedom and creativity.

The bird gives the duet its flair, bringing fresh ideas, energy, and excitement.

The hippo gives the duet its foundation, providing stability, consistency, and security.

Much like Emma and Adam's marriage, the bird and the hippo show us that differences in marriage aren't obstacles—they're opportunities to create a more beautiful harmony.

When each partner learns to respect and celebrate the other's song, they move beyond clashing tunes and into a duet that reflects the richness of their partnership.

Chapter 9 Reflection Questions

What are your personal dreams, and how do they align with your marriage?

How can you better support your spouse's purpose while pursuing your own?

What shared vision could you create to guide your marriage toward God's purpose?

CHAPTER 10

Your Love Is the Sermon Everyone's Watching

Marriage is more than two people sharing a last name, a Netflix account, or navigating thermostat debates. It's a living, breathing reflection of God's love in action. A strong, Christ-centered marriage demonstrates the Gospel, revealing the fruits of the Spirit—love, joy, peace, patience, kindness, goodness, faithfulness, gentleness, and self-control—woven together with grace, forgiveness, sacrifice, and unshakable joy. When others witness this unity, they see the transformative power of the Gospel alive in a dynamic, God-ordained partnership.

But let's be real: sometimes, "marriage as ministry" feels more like marriage as survival. How can a couple navigate the messy, mundane moments of life while staying focused on the bigger picture, using their relationship to glorify God and serve others?

Rachel and Caleb were the golden couple at church. They taught Sunday school, volunteered for every outreach event, and always seemed to have it together. But behind closed doors, their marriage was in trouble. Caleb felt burnt out from constantly saying yes to ministry obligations. Rachel, feeling unsupported, resented Caleb's emotional distance.

One Saturday morning, after a particularly tense argument, Rachel blurted, "How can we lead others when we can't even figure out our own marriage?"

Caleb looked at her and said, "Maybe that's the problem. We're trying to lead instead of letting God lead us."

The Lightkeeper

Imagine a lighthouse. Its purpose is to guide others toward safety, but if the lightkeeper doesn't tend the flame, the lighthouse becomes useless in the fog. Rachel and Caleb were so busy shining for others that they neglected their own flame. In ministry and marriage, you can't pour into others if your cup is empty.

Ministry starts at home. Galatians 6:10 reminds us, *As we have opportunity, let us do good to all people, especially to those who belong to the family of believers.* Your spouse is your first ministry. A healthy marriage is a powerful testimony. In John 13:35, Jesus says, *By this everyone will know that you are my disciples if you love one another.* Your love for each other speaks louder than words.

After their conversation, Rachel and Caleb decided to step back from some of their church obligations to focus on their marriage. They started setting boundaries around their time, and intentionally reconnecting. To their surprise, their authenticity about the struggles they faced became a more powerful ministry than their perfect façade.

Making Your Marriage a Ministry

Spiritual intimacy strengthens your bond and sets an example for others. Start with simple prayers and build from there.

Whether it's volunteering at church, mentoring younger couples, or hosting small groups, find ways to serve as a team.

You don't need to pretend your marriage is perfect. Every couple faces conflict. How you handle disagreements—offering forgiveness and seeking reconciliation—can inspire others to do the same. \Sharing your challenges (and how you overcome them) will encourage others.

Attend marriage retreats, read books together, and seek mentorship from older, godly couples. A strong marriage equips you to serve others better.

A Marriage the Reflects and Revels

Marriage is an old mirror and a window at the same time, working together to show both the internal and external beauty of a relationship built on love, faith, and grace. The mirror reflects God's love within the marriage, a reminder to both partners to extend grace, practice patience, and walk humbly with one another. The window allows others to look in, to see how God is working through your union as a testimony of His love.

But here's the catch: if the mirror becomes dirty—clouded by resentment, neglect, or pride—the window becomes cloudy too. What happens inside the marriage ultimately shapes what others see from the outside.

The mirror represents what happens between the two of

you—the internal dynamics of your marriage. It reflects:

Your Communication: Are your words kind and constructive, or sharp and dismissive?

Your Attitude: Do you act with respect and consideration, or do you let irritation and impatience take over?

Your Faith: Do you pray together, encourage each other spiritually, and lean on Him during challenges?

The mirror is a constant reminder to see your spouse—and yourself—through the lens of God's grace. Just as Christ forgives and loves us despite our flaws, the mirror calls you to love your spouse with the same grace.

But what happens when the mirror is dirty?

Resentment can cloud it. Instead of seeing your spouse through the eyes of love, you only see their mistakes and shortcomings.

Pride can distort it. Instead of reflecting humility, it becomes a source of blame or self-righteousness.

Neglect can fog it. If you stop nurturing your connection, the reflection dims, and you lose sight of the love and grace that once defined your relationship.

The window represents how your marriage is perceived by others—your children, friends, family, and even your community. A healthy marriage shines as an example of God's love, offering hope and encouragement to those who see it.

Through the window, others witness:

Your Unity: How you work together as a team, navigating life's challenges with mutual support.

Your Forgiveness: How you reconcile after conflicts, showing that love is stronger than pride.

Your Joy: The laughter, peace, and connection that comes from a marriage rooted in God's love.

The window isn't about projecting perfection—it's about authenticity. It shows that while your marriage isn't flawless, it's real, grounded in faith, and constantly growing.

But what happens when the window is cloudy?

If the mirror is neglected, the love and grace that should shine through the window are obscured. Children may see a marriage full of tension rather than tenderness, shaping their view of relationships. Friends and family may sense distance instead of unity, making it harder to see God's hand at work.

Keeping the Mirror Clean

Daily Reflection:

Take time each day to reflect on how you've treated your spouse. Did your words and actions reflect love, patience, and humility? If not, take steps to apologize and make amends.

Regular Maintenance:

Just like cleaning a real mirror, maintaining the emotional and spiritual health of your marriage requires consistent effort. Pray together, spend quality time, and prioritize open communication.

Acknowledge the Smudges:

Don't ignore small issues. Resentment and pride build up like fingerprints on a mirror. Address conflicts quickly and with a spirit of reconciliation.

Keeping the WIndow Clear

Be Authentic:

The window doesn't need to show perfection—it needs to show authenticity. Let your children, friends, and community see how you handle struggles with grace and perseverance.

Shine Together:

Serve together, worship together, and create a culture of love and unity in your home. Let the window show that God's love is the foundation of your marriage.

Consider Your Legacy:

Remember that your marriage is a living example to others. How you treat one another shapes the faith and relationships of those watching.

How the Mirror and Window are Connected

The state of your mirror determines what others see through the window. If your marriage is full of love, grace, and humility, the window will naturally reflect those qualities, offering hope and inspiration. But if the mirror is neglected, the window becomes clouded, and the beauty of God's work in your marriage becomes harder to see.

Marriage isn't just about the two of you—it's about how your relationship reflects God's love to a world that desperately needs to see it. By keeping your mirror clean and your window clear, your marriage becomes both a private sanctuary of grace and a public testimony of faith.

So ask yourself: Is your mirror reflecting God's love in your marriage? And is your window allowing others to see His hand at work? If not, it's never too late to start cleaning. After all, a clear mirror and a bright window can turn any marriage into a beacon of light and hope.

And remember, your marriage doesn't have to be perfect to be powerful. When you let God lead, even your struggles can become a testimony of His grace. So tend your lighthouse, clean your mirror, and let your love be the sermon everyone's binge watching.

Chapter 10 Reflection Questions

How does your marriage reflect God's love to others?

How can you use your marriage to encourage and support others in their faith journey?

What steps can you take to serve your spouse as your first ministry?

CHAPTER 11

Because the World Needs More Leaders (and Fewer Juice Boxes)

It's Monday morning, and the kitchen is a war zone.

Seven-year-old Mason is yelling, "That's MY juice box!" while his five-year-old sister, defiantly clutches it like a prize trophy.

Meanwhile, their parents, are trying to mediate with coffee in one hand and half-burnt toast in the other.

"Why can't they just share?" Chris mutters. Danielle replies, "Because they're children—and this is how to survive juice box wars."

Raising children is training kings and queens for their future thrones. You're not just parenting for today, you're equipping your kids with the values, skills, and faith they'll need to rule their own households and impact the world. Proverbs 22:6 reminds us,

> *Train up a child in the way he should go, and*
> *when he is old, he will not depart from it.*

Your home is their first kingdom, and how you lead as parents shapes the kind of leaders they'll become.

God's Blueprint for Parenting

Parenting is like tending a garden, a shared responsibility between God and the parents, with each plant (child) requiring its own care. Some plants thrive in sunlight, others need shade. Some grow quickly, while others take years to bear fruit. But all plants need nurturing to flourish.

The garden represents your family. You and your spouse are the gardeners, tasked with cultivating a space where every child can grow strong and rooted in God's love. The tools you use, faith, discipline, grace, and wisdom, shape the health of your garden. And just like a garden, the process isn't quick or easy, but the harvest is worth the effort.

In today's world, your garden might look different. Perhaps you're co-parenting in a blended family, raising children who identify differently than traditional roles, or managing relationships with adult children. No matter the type of garden you're tending to, the principles of love, care, and faith remain the same.

Every Plant Grows Differently

Like a garden with multiple species, each child may come from a different background, requiring unique care. One child might need more discipline, while another thrives on affirmation. Recognize their individual needs instead of treating them all the same. Older plants still need attention. Pruning, fertilizing, and providing occasional shade (or advice) help them thrive while honoring their independence.

Children, regardless of age, need strong roots. If the soil (home environment) is rocky, the roots struggle to take hold. In blended families, creating this foundation might take extra effort. Building trust, showing consistency, and treating every child with equal love cultivates a sense of belonging.

Discipline is the pruning—it shapes growth and removes what's harmful. However, too much pruning can stunt growth, while neglecting it can lead to overgrowth and chaos. Grace is the balance. When Mason forgot to clean up his mess, Danielle chose to teach instead of scold. She explained the importance of leadership and teamwork in keeping the "garden" (home) healthy. What you cultivate inside prepares them for life beyond the family garden.

Assign age-appropriate chores. Just as every gardener tends their patch of the garden, every family member should have a role. For Taylor, it meant contributing financially to groceries. For Mason and Ava, it was about sharing responsibilities like feeding the dog or doing dishes.

A healthy garden requires selflessness. Show your children that leadership means serving others, just as Jesus washed His disciples' feet (John 13:14-15). For Chris, this looked like stepping into conflicts with fairness, even when it would've been easier to take sides.

Weeds are inevitable in every garden. They represent challenges—resentment, misunderstandings, or even outside influences. Left unchecked, they can choke out healthy growth.Danielle and Chris faced weeds of jealousy between Mason and Taylor. Mason felt like Taylor received more grace because of her adult status, while Taylor struggled with feeling like she was walking on eggshells around her younger siblings.

To address the weeds, do three things:

Pull Them Out at the Root: Don't let feelings fester. Encourage open conversations, asking each child to share their perspective.

Apply the Right Tools: Instead of favoring one over the other, lean on Scripture to guide fairness and grace, showing how God's love is abundant enough for everyone.

Expand the Garden: Embracing Diversity

In some families, the garden might include children who identify outside traditional gender roles or LGBTQ+ family members. While this can challenge traditional perspectives, the call to love and nurture remains the same.

For parents facing these situations, remember:

> You are the gardener, but God is the Creator. Trust Him to guide you as you care for your children.
>
> Growth takes time. Be patient as you and your family navigate new dynamics.

Love is the foundation. Regardless of identity or circumstances, your role is to reflect God's love consistently.

Tending to your family's garden is a lifelong responsibility, requiring discernment, flexibility, and faith. Every garden faces challenges—weather changes, pests, weeds, and the natural differences between plants. Similarly, every family must navigate external pressures, internal conflicts, and individual needs while staying rooted in God's love and wisdom.

Ensuring Your Garden Thrives

1. Understand the Seasons of Growth

Gardens go through seasons, and so do children and families. Recognizing these seasons can help you adjust your approach to nurturing your family.

Spring (Early Childhood): This is the planting phase. It's a time for laying down roots of faith, love, and discipline. Children are like tender sprouts, soaking up everything around them.

What to Do: Provide a safe, structured environment. Use consistent discipline and introduce faith in simple, age-appropriate ways (bedtime prayers, Bible stories).

Summer (Adolescence): Growth is rapid, but this season can bring storms. Teens push boundaries as they develop their independence, much like plants that grow wild if left untended.

What to Do: Balance freedom with guidance. Provide boundaries without smothering growth. Focus on conversations that help them connect faith to their choices.

Autumn (Young Adulthood): This is the harvesting phase. Your children begin to make their own decisions, and you start to see the fruit of what you've sown.

What to Do: Offer wisdom without overstepping. Celebrate their accomplishments and give them the tools to weather life's challenges independently.

Winter (Adult Children): Even mature plants need care. Adult children often return to the family garden during hard times, or they need support as they start their own gardens.

What to Do: Be a steady presence. Provide advice and encouragement but respect their independence.

2. Different Plants, Different Needs

No two children are alike, even if they grow up in the same household. Like plants in a garden, each child has unique needs, temperaments, and purposes.

High-Maintenance Plants (Children Who Need Extra Support): Some kids struggle more with school, emotions, or social skills. These children require more patience and care.

What to Do: Offer extra attention without showing favoritism. Equip them with resources like counseling, tutoring, or mentorship, and remind them that their struggles don't define their worth.

Self-Sufficient Plants (Independent or Overachieving Kids): These kids may seem like they don't need much care, but they often struggle with hidden pressures.

What to Do: Praise their efforts, not just their outcomes. Create opportunities for them to rest and remind them it's okay to ask for help.

New Additions (Blended Families or Adopted Kids): New members in the garden may struggle to find their place or feel different.

What to Do: Build trust through consistency and inclusion. Make an effort to understand their background and incorporate their unique traits into the family culture.

3. Protect Against Pests and Weeds

Pests and weeds in the garden symbolize the challenges that threaten to derail your family's growth. These might be negative influences, unresolved conflicts, or harmful habits.

Negative Influences: Friends, media, or cultural pressures can plant "weeds" of doubt, insecurity, or rebellion in your children.

What to Do: Monitor your child's environment. Teach them to discern what aligns with God's truth without being overly controlling.

Unresolved Conflicts: Tension between family members can choke out healthy relationships.

What to Do: Address issues quickly and with grace. Model forgiveness and encourage open communication.

Harmful Habits: Over-scheduling, poor boundaries, or a lack of discipline can lead to burnout and chaos.

What to Do: Create a balanced schedule. Prioritize family time and teach the importance of rest and reflection.

4. Focus on the Soil

Good soil is foundational for growth. If the environment is toxic, even the healthiest plants will struggle. Create a family culture that nourishes faith, love, and respect.

Foster Open Communication: Make your home a place where everyone feels safe to express their thoughts and feelings without fear of judgment.

Encourage Family Worship: Set aside time to pray, read Scripture, and worship together. This keeps your family rooted in God's truth.

Model Grace and Forgiveness: Show your children how to resolve conflict in a way that honors God.

5. Be Patient with Growth

Gardens don't grow overnight, and neither do children. Patience is one of the most important virtues for parents.

Celebrate Small Wins: Don't wait for major milestones to affirm your children. Celebrate their effort, growth, and character along the way.

Trust God's Timing: You may not see the fruits of your labor immediately but remember that God is always at work behind the scenes.

6. Leave Room for God's Hand

As gardeners, parents can plant seeds, water the soil, and protect against threats, but only God can make things grow.

Trusting Him with the process is essential.

Surrender Control: Release the need to micromanage your children's growth. Trust God to work in their lives in ways you can't.

Pray for Wisdom: Parenting is hard, and there's no one-size-fits- all approach. Ask God for the wisdom to handle challenges with grace and discernment.

7. Prepare Your Children for Their Own Gardens

Your goal as a parent isn't just to raise good kids—it's to prepare them to cultivate their own gardens someday. Teach them how to apply faith, resilience, and love in their own lives so they can thrive as adults and maybe even parents.

Teach Life Skills: Equip your children with practical skills like managing money, resolving conflicts, and making grounded and researched decisions.

Model Healthy Relationships: Let your marriage or partnership serve as an example of what mutual respect and love look like, remember the mirror and window.

Independence: Gradually give your children more responsibility, teaching them to rely on God as they grow.

Cultivatinga Legacy

A well-tended garden doesn't just benefit the plants in it — it becomes a source of nourishment and beauty for others. As you tend your family's garden, you're not just raising children—you're cultivating a legacy that will bless generations to come.

You're not gardening alone. God is your master gardener, guiding you through every season, providing strength during storms, and ensuring that the seeds you plant will still yield fruit in His perfect timing.

CHAPTER 12
The Theater vs. The Director's Cut

In your blockbuster movie, people see the edited, polished version that makes it to the big screen. The theater cut, the version everyone else watches, is filled with highlights: smiling family photos, anniversary celebrations, or sweet captions about how much you love each other. It's what the world sees, a curated collection of moments that tell part of the story.

But the director's cut? That's where the real magic happens. It's raw, unfiltered, and unapologetically authentic. It's the behind-the-scenes footage that shows the tears, the mistakes, the awkward pauses, and the unglamorous realities that make a marriage real. It's the version that reveals the work, the patience, and the grace required to create something lasting.

The theater version may draw applause, but the director's cut is where you find the truth—the deep, messy, and transformative journey of two people learning to love each other as God intended.

Theater cuts are for the audience. They're crafted to please, impress, or entertain. But the director's cut is for the creators—it's the version that captures the full vision of the story. In marriage, the director's cut isn't about performing for others; it's about living out the covenant between you, your spouse, and God.

Theater Version: A curated highlight reel designed to look perfect. It glosses over conflict, struggles, and growth.

Example: Posting a smiling photo from date night, even though you argued in the car on the way there.

Director's Cut: The authentic version that includes every take, retake, and blooper. It's the version where you see God working through the challenges to create a masterpiece.

Example: The argument in the car becomes a breakthrough moment where you both learn to listen and understand each other better.

Behind the Scenes

The director's cut reminds us that the most meaningful parts of marriage aren't always pretty, but they're always purposeful.

The Bloopers

Every marriage has its share of bloopers, forgotten anniversaries, mismatched expectations, and poorly timed jokes. These moments may not make it to the theater version, but they're integral to the director's cut. Why do they matter? Great Question! Bloopers remind us to laugh at ourselves, to find joy

in the imperfections, and to see grace in the moments that don't go as planned.

The Retakes

In a theater version, the final scene is perfect. In the director's cut, you see the countless retakes it took to get there. Every disagreement that led to reconciliation, every failed attempt at understanding that eventually turned into growth, is part of the process. Why do retakes matter? Again, great question! Retakes are where growth happens. They show us that love isn't about getting it right the first time; it's about showing up again and again until the story reflects God's vision.

The Unscripted Moments

The best parts of any story often aren't scripted—they're spontaneous, raw, and real. In marriage, these moments are the unexpected gestures, the unplanned sacrifices, and the quiet acts of love that no one else sees. The unscripted moments matter because they reveal the heart of your marriage: love expressed not in grand gestures, but in small, consistent acts of care and devotion.

The Ultimate Director

In every great film, the director has the vision—the big picture of how all the scenes, characters, and moments fit together. In marriage, God is the ultimate director. He sees the story you're building, not just the polished scenes but the raw footage, too.

The fights, the laughter, the silences, and the celebrations—God uses it all to shape your story. Romans 8:28 reminds us,

And we know that in all things God works for the good of those who love him, who have been called according to his purpose.

When we get lost in the day-to-day struggles, God sees how it all comes together. He knows that the director's cut of your marriage is a masterpiece in progress. The funny thing is what we see as a mistake, God sees as an opportunity. Even the worst moments in your marriage can be used to bring you closer together and closer to Him.

Performing for the Audiance

It's tempting to make your marriage look perfect for others, but true fulfillment comes from living authentically with your spouse. Stop worrying abouwhat others see and focus on what God is building in your relationship. The hard conversations, the sacrifices, the forgiveness—they're all part of the story. Don't hide these moments; embrace them as evidence of God's work in your marriage. Even when you don't understand the scene you're in, trust that God is weaving it into a bigger picture.

Theater versions may win awards or social media likes, but director's cuts change lives. Your marriage isn't meant to impress others, even though they are watching; it's meant to reflect God's love, grace, and purpose. It's meant to be real, raw, and redemptive.

The director's cut of your marriage isn't polished or perfect—it's honest, transformative, and filled with God's fingerprints.

And that's what makes it a masterpiece worth living.

In the end, the final scene plays. It's not flashy or dramatic —it's a simple moment, like sitting on a porch swing together, watching the sunset. The couple, older and weathered but full of peace, smiles as they reflect on the journey. The camera pans back, revealing that their marriage wasn't just about them. The impact of their love ripples outward—to their children, their community, and even strangers who witnessed their faithfulness.

And then the screen fades to black, with one line appearing,

Well done, my good and faithful servant. (Matthew 25:23)

Chapter 12 Reflection Questions

What parts of your marriage are you tempted to hide in the theater version?

How can you embrace the "bloopers" and "retakes" as part of God's work in your story?

Are you trusting God's vision for your marriage, even when the current scene feels messy or incomplete?

CHAPTER 13

Why Your Love Language Lied to You
(and Why That's a Good Thing)

Love languages promise clarity in the chaotic world of relationships. They're simple, relatable, and powerful tools for understanding how people give and receive love. But here's the problem: too often, we treat them as the solution instead of what they are—a starting point.

Your love language didn't lie maliciously; it told you the truth about what makes you feel seen, valued, and appreciated. But it left out something critical: love languages alone can't sustain a relationship. They're not the summit of love but the first step in climbing higher. In this chapter, we'll explore how to use your love language as a ladder, moving from preference to purpose, from satisfaction to sacrifice.

The Love Ladder

Your love language is the bottom rung of a ladder. It's where you start, data about what resonates most deeply with you or your partner. But if you stay on the bottom rung, you miss the opportunity to climb higher toward something more profound, growth, transformation, and spiritual intimacy.

Here's how each love language can become a ladder for relational growth, helping you climb beyond comfort into deeper connection.

1. Words of Affirmation: Moving from Flattery to Truth

People who crave words of affirmation want their partner to articulate love, encouragement, and appreciation. A well-placed compliment can light up their world. The Danger is words can become hollow. If the actions behind them don't align, they're reduced to empty flattery.

You can use affirmation to build a foundation of truth-telling and accountability. Affirm not just your partner's achievements but their struggles, character, and growth.

Instead of just saying, "I love how you handled that," dive deeper and try, "I see how hard this is for you, and I'm proud of the effort you're putting in. It inspires me to do better, too." *Therefore, encourage one another and build each other up, just as, in fact, you are doing* - 1 Thessalonians 5:11. True affirmation doesn't just make someone feel good; it calls them higher.

2. Acts of Service: From Doing Tasks to Sacrificial Love

Acts of service say, "I love you enough to make your load lighter." It's about actions speaking louder than words. The danger is acts of service can become transactional or resentful — "I do for you, so you should do for me." Transform service into sacrificial love that mirrors Christ's humility. Instead of focusing on tasks, focus on presence. It's not about doing everything perfectly but about being fully present even when you're tired or overwhelmed. *The greatest among you will be your servant* - Matthew 23:11. Love through service reflects the heart of Christ when it comes from a place of joy, not obligation.

3. Receiving Gifts: From Tokens to Treasures

For some, tangible expressions of love, a gift, or a thoughtful gesture communicate deep care. The danger is gifts can be misinterpreted as materialism or lose meaning if they're not thoughtful. Shift from giving things to creating moments and meaning. Instead of focusing on the object, focus on what it symbolizes.

A handwritten note with the gift that explains why it matters or a gift of time, like planning an intentional day together. Every good and perfect gift is from above - James 1:17. Gifts are meaningful when they reflect the heart and intention behind them.

4. Quality Time: From Proximity to Presence

People who value quality time crave undivided attention and shared experiences. It's about prioritizing connection over distractions. The danger is time together can feel empty if it's not intentional or if emotional walls remain. Turn quality time into sacred time that fosters intimacy.

Go beyond spending time together; engage in deeper conversations that reveal your partner's heart. Instead of just watching TV, ask, "What's something you've been thinking about lately that you haven't shared?" This creates thought and intimacy while spending time. Where two or three gather in my name, there am I with them - Matthew 18:20. Time becomes transformative when it's infused with purpose and your full presence.

5. Physical Touch: From Contact to Connection

Physical touch reassures and affirms. It's about the power of closeness to communicate love without words. The danger is touch can become routine, losing its ability to convey intimacy. Move from habitual touch to healing touch. Use physical touch as a way to convey safety, vulnerability, and affection. Holding hands during prayer or using touch to comfort during conflict, not just during romantic moments. *Jesus reached out his hand and touched the man* - Matthew 8:3. Touch is a sacred act of connection, not just affection.

A Shared Love Language

While individuals in a marriage often have their own primary love languages, developing a shared love language offers couples a unique opportunity to express their connection A shared love language goes beyond individual preferences, symbolizing the growth, creativity, and teamwork that define a thriving relationship. Much like the hippo and the bird, whose differing strengths and expressions complement each other, a shared love language becomes a bridge that unites two distinct personalities.

A shared love language deepens connection by fostering a sense of " we" rather than "me and you." It represents the couple's ability to create something together that neither could achieve alone. For instance, the hippo and the bird might discover a shared ritual of sitting by the river each evening, where the bird sings softly while the hippo rests. This blend of the bird's expressive energy and the hippo's grounded nature creates a moment that belongs uniquely to them, transforming a simple activity into a powerful expression of love.

Creating a shared love language also strengthens resilience. In challenging times, this shared expression can serve as a grounding force, reminding couples of their unity and shared purpose. According to Gottman and Silver (2015), positive rituals and habits in relationships help couples navigate difficulties by reinforcing connection and trust. For the hippo and the bird, their shared ritual of a quiet evening together might become a way to realign when their differences create tension, offering a safe and predictable moment to rebuild intimacy.

This process often enhances creativity in expressing love.

Couples are encouraged to think beyond traditional expressions and blend their unique dynamics into something meaningful. Like the hippo's preference for acts of service and the bird's love for quality time, couples can combine their love languages into rituals that reflect both their needs. For example, preparing a meal together might satisfy one partner's need for teamwork and the other's desire for connection, merging two distinct expressions into one shared language.

Developing a shared love language often begins with recognizing patterns in the relationship, such as activities or routines that already bring both partners joy. For the hippo and the bird, these might include their shared moments of teamwork during river crossings or their enjoyment of sunsets together.

Over time, these patterns can evolve into traditions, such as a nightly prayer, a weekly walk, or a shared hobby, that celebrate their bond and strengthen their connection.

Ultimately, shared love languages enhance the uniqueness of the couple's bond. Just as the hippo and the bird have created a partnership that is stronger because of their differences, a shared love language allows couples to celebrate their union in a way that resonates deeply and personally. These shared expressions of love often become a legacy, inspiring others and offering stability and joy within the relationship. By creating something together that is uniquely theirs, couples honor their story, much like the hippo and the bird who build a life that neither could create alone.

Data, not Doctorine

Love languages reveal preferences—they give you valuable data about how you or your partner feel most loved. But they're not the destination; they're tools to help you build a deeper relationship to reach the destination.

The reason a love language is not enough is because love must evolve. Your needs and your partner's needs will change over time. Staying stuck in one language limits growth. The ultimate goal is not to meet preferences but to grow in humility, grace, and Christ-like love.

Yes, use the love languages to understand each other better. However, use what you've learned to deepen your connection and foster growth while you aim for transformation. Use your partner's language to help your relationship reflect the sacrificial, unconditional love at the top of the ladder.

Your love languages didn't lie to you; they just didn't tell you the whole truth. Love isn't about staying comfortable—it's about climbing higher, moving farther, and growing deeper. By using the love languages as tools, not as the final solution, you can build a relationship that doesn't just speak love but lives it.

Chapter 13 Reflection Questions

Which love language resonates most with you? Why do you think it matters to you so much?

Have there been times when your love language didn't feel "enough" in your relationship? What was missing?

How well do you know your partner's love language? How often do you intentionally act on it?

Think of a time when you focused on your partner's love language but still felt disconnected. What deeper needs or emotions might have been at play?

What are you currently doing to climb beyond the love languages in your relationship?

Love Language Audit

Sit with your partner and write down your top love language and theirs. Discuss:

How often do you feel your love language is fulfilled?

What's one thing your partner has done recently that truly made you feel loved?

What's one thing you could do to fulfill their love language better?

Write down one action each of you will take this week to speak the other's love language more intentionally.

CHAPTER 14
From This Day Forward

The hippo and the bird had come a long way since their first cautious steps toward collaboration. Their differences, once sources of frustration, had become the very foundation of their partnership. The bird's vision lifted them to new heights, while the hippo's strength kept them grounded. Together, they had built a life that was as colorful and dynamic as the sunsets they now watched side by side.

One evening, as they rested near the riverbank, the bird said, "Remember when we argued about crossing the river? I thought you were too cautious, and you thought I was too reckless." The hippo chuckled, his deep voice rumbling like the river itself. "And now we've crossed so many rivers, I've lost count."

Their journey had not been without its challenges. There were days when the bird felt weighed down by the hippo's steady, deliberate pace and moments when the hippo felt overwhelmed by the bird's endless curiosity. Yet, each challenge taught them how to lean into each other's strengths instead of pulling away. They learned that marriage, like their journey, was not about being perfect but about persevering together.

A Marriage that Thrives

As the sun dipped below the horizon, casting a golden glow over the water, the bird and the hippo reflected on the principles that had guided them:

They learned to speak openly about their needs and fears, creating a safe space for vulnerability. The hippo's steady listening balanced the bird's fluttering thoughts, and the bird's gentle encouragement drew the hippo out of his shell.

Instead of resenting their contrasting natures, they embraced them. The bird brought spontaneity and creativity to the hippo's world, while the hippo provided a solid foundation for the bird's dreams.

They discovered the joy of putting each other's needs above their own. When the hippo felt stuck, the bird would soar above and find a new path. When the bird felt weary, the hippo would carry her safely on his back.

They realized that their union was strongest when they relied not just on each other but also on the divine design that brought them together. Prayer, empowerment, and wisdom became their anchors.

A Marriage Worth Aspiring To

If you didn't know by now, this story is not just about a hippo and a bird. It's about you and your partner, navigating the complexities of marriage. It's about realizing that love is not always easy but always worth it. Like the hippo and the bird, you may find that your greatest challenges become your greatest strengths when approached with humility, grace, and a commitment to growth. Remember this:

When differences arise, let them draw you closer rather than push you apart.

Practice Forgiveness: Every misstep is an opportunity to repair and rebuild, adding depth to your story.

Build a Legacy Together: Your marriage is not just for today; it's a foundation for future generations to learn from and aspire to.

The Adventure Continues

As night fell, the hippo and the bird prepared to rest, knowing that tomorrow would bring new rivers to cross and new adventures to share. "We've come so far," the bird said softly, nestling against the hippo's side.

"And we've got so much further to go," the hippo replied with a smile.

Their story doesn't end here, and neither does yours. As you close this book, think of the rivers still waiting for you to cross, the skies still calling you to explore, and the strength within you to walk side by side. The hippo and the bird found their rhythm, not by striving to be the same but by embracing the beauty of their differences.

From this day forward, may you step into your marriage with courage and grace. From this day forward build together, dream together, and carry each other when the road gets rough. From this day forward, when the sun sets on your journey, may you look back and say, "We were better together, and we made it through—together."

Your story, like theirs, is just beginning!

From this day forward, may your marriage soar to new heights and remain as steady as the riverbanks you build upon. From this day forward.

CONCLUSION

As this journey through the pages of marriage comes to an end, I hope it's just the beginning of a renewed chapter in your relationship. Marriage is not a static destination; it's a dynamic, evolving partnership shaped by love, patience, and faith. Like the hippo and the bird, every couple must navigate life's rivers together—sometimes wading through challenges, sometimes soaring to new heights, but always moving forward hand in hand.

This book is not a prescription but an invitation—an invitation to look at your marriage with fresh eyes, to embrace the beauty of your differences, and to commit to building a legacy of love that reflects the best of what you and your spouse can be. Whether your journey is just beginning or decades in, know that every step taken in grace, humility, and intention strengthens the bond you share.

I encourage you to take the lessons, reflections, and practical tools from these chapters and make them your own. Revisit them in seasons of joy and struggle alike. Share them with others who may need encouragement in their marriages. And above all, remember that love, rooted in faith and nurtured by action, has the power to transform not only your relationship but also the lives you touch together.

Your marriage is a gift—not just to each other but to the world. Treat it with care, celebrate its uniqueness, and never stop striving to make it as vibrant and unshakable as the union you dreamed of when you first said, "I do."

From this day forward, may your love continue to grow, your partnership deepens, and your story inspire others to believe in the beauty of marriage.

With gratitude and hope,

Timothy Hunter

ABOUT THE AUTHOR

Timothy Hunter is a distinguished Behavioral Health Specialist and Wellness Coach, dedicated to guiding individuals toward holistic well-being. With a robust background in behavioral health, he has authored five insightful books that blend spiritual wisdom with practical strategies for personal growth.

As the founder of Pew 13, Timothy offers a unique approach to wellness, emphasizing the integration of prayer, empowerment, and wisdom. His platform provides behavior management and life skills training, focusing on areas such as interpersonal communication, self-help, safety, and daily living skills. Through support, observation, intervention, and redirection, he assists individuals in overcoming challenges and achieving their goals.

Timothy's engaging presence extends to social media, where he hosts Pew TV on YouTube, and Pew13 on all social media sites. His content resonates with a diverse audience, offering guidance and support in behavioral health and personal development.

Committed to the belief that spirituality and actionable steps are essential for personal transformation, Timothy encourages individuals to couple their faith with practical efforts to create goals that are specific, manageable, effective, reliable, and trustworthy. His work continues to inspire and empower those seeking to navigate life's challenges with resilience and faith.

www.ingramcontent.com/pod-product-compliance
Lightning Source LLC
Chambersburg PA
CBHW071545220526
45469CB00003B/923